Twelve Modern Scottish Poets

Twelve Modern Scottish Poets

edited by
Charles King

LION LIBRARY
London   Toronto   Sydney

Copyright © Charles King, 1971

First published in the United Kingdom
by University of London Press Ltd., 1971

*Also available in paperback from
Hodder & Stoughton Ltd.*

First Lion Library edition, 1974
Second Lion Library edition, 1976

ISBN 0 7082 0025 7

Made and printed in Great Britain
for White Lion Publishers Ltd.,
138 Park Lane, London, W1Y 3DD

CONTENTS

6

PREFACE

Since the unitary British Empire became the fissiparous Commonwealth of Nations, the literary and academic worlds have gradually accustomed themselves to the concept of a number of English literatures – that of England itself, Commonwealth, American, Anglo-Irish literatures, to name only the most familiar. Each must be studied in terms of its own social, political and cultural history. Scottish literature is at once the closest to, and the most distant from, the native English tradition; the closest, as the result of geographical continuity and close political assimilation; the most distant, partly because the Scottish social environment and national history is so distinct from that of England, but even more because only in Scotland and the south-eastern midlands of England did the English language develop forms accepted over wide areas and for long periods as literary standards. The Scottish standard dominated the imaginative literature of the fifteenth and much of the sixteenth centuries: it came close to dominating that of the later eighteenth and earlier nineteenth centuries. Within that standard, the achievement of the twentieth century is lesser, perhaps, but impressive and far-ranging.

From the fifteenth century to the present day, Scottish authors have also written in the other standard of southern English. The earlier successes for the most part were in prose – one thinks of Knox, Hume, Boswell, Scott and Carlyle – but the poetic achievement was not negligible. James I of Scotland, William Drummond and the earlier James Thomson by any standards are worthwhile poets. 'The Kingis Quair', Drummond's Baptist sonnet, or Thomson's 'Winter' (in many ways so reminiscent of Gavin Douglas's Prologue to his translation of *Aeneid* VII) belong to the full Scottish tradition in almost the same way as the 'Bruce', the 'Testament of Cresseid' or 'Tam o' Shanter'. The twentieth century has seen the widening and deepening of this mode of writing.

I speak of poets writing in one or other of the two standards, but there is no simple artistic necessity for any poet to confine himself to either. The quality of some at least among Burns's English poems is at last being recognised; a lesser poet, R. L. Stevenson, was sometimes able to write memorably in Scots as well as English. Dr C. M. Grieve is the pre-eminent example of a twentieth-century Scots poet able to utilise the resources of both standards.

Mr King has extended his anthology to cover poems by twentieth-century poets writing in either or both standards. In order to provide representative selections, he has limited himself to twelve poets. The result is a fascinating and rewarding volume. It will be an excellent thing for literary studies in general if Mr King finds a wide audience in Scotland and elsewhere. I wish him all success.

JOHN MACQUEEN
School of Scottish Studies
University of Edinburgh

INTRODUCTION

The Modern Scottish Literary Renaissance has been widely recognised as starting with the early poetry of Hugh MacDiarmid in *Sangschaw* and *Penny Wheep* (1926) but notably with the appearance of the explosive *A Drunk Man Looks at the Thistle* in 1926. Since that time the literary movement has gained such impetus that today Scottish poetry is accepted once more as an important force in literature. Still the wider reading public of Scotland hardly knows of the existence of its poets. The cost of a single volume of poems by even the most recognised of poets is so considerable that it is impossible without either a particular enthusiasm or unusual opportunity for readers to know to any extent the works of any living Scottish poet.

Anthologies of modern Scottish verse certainly have appeared from time to time since the end of the 1939-45 war but have generally presented slender offerings from a wide field, with random samples even from outstanding poets. It seemed to the present editor and his committee that it was time for an anthology which would present a significant selection of poems from a limited range of established poets. This book should contain for each author a considerable body of poems with an introductory essay on the poet, notes for the more difficult poems and glosses for poems in Scots. The selection of poets presented many difficulties. As the anthology is intended to be suitable for upper school and college, teachability has been an important factor in the selection. After reading the works of more than forty poets, a *leet* of some twenty was drawn up from which the chosen twelve emerged.

Scotland has three recognised tongues – English, Scots and Gaelic, all having valid claims for presentation in the anthology.

With much regret, because of lack of space, it was decided that poems in Gaelic must be omitted, although one of the writers represented here, Iain Crichton Smith, has earned a considerable reputation for his Gaelic poetry. The name of an outstanding and influential Gaelic poet, Sorley Maclean, must be mentioned and I cannot refrain from quoting here one brief poem from his volume, *Dain Do Eimhir* (translated by Iain Crichton Smith), an eloquent reply to a pronouncement by Yeats:

'The innocent and the beautiful have no enemy but time.' Yeats

> I thought I understood from you
> that these lines were exact and true
> Nor did I think that I would find
> their falsehood bitter in my mind.
>
> But that plausible epigram
> proved itself another dream
> When on that Monday I saw with dread
> the steel helmet on your golden head.'

Scots is more accessible to the modern reader, particularly where glosses are provided, and so poetry in Scots has an important place in the anthology.

The dozen poets finally selected, except for two, are still alive and as this work goes to press, are all actively writing. In general they represent the various regions of Scotland: MacDiarmid is poet of the Scottish Borders; Muir and Mackay Brown are from the Orkney Islands; Crichton Smith from the Hebrides; George Bruce and Alexander Scott from the North-east; Edwin Morgan comes from Glasgow, Soutar from Perth, and Tom Scott represents St Andrews, while Robert Garioch, Norman MacCaig and Sydney Goodsir Smith are distinctly poets of Edinburgh. All have something essentially Scottish about themselves and also about their work. A study of their poetry must increase the awareness of the reader of what has given Scotland its particular identity. While Iain Crichton Smith is constantly aware of the restricting effect on the artist of a Hebridean background, George Mackay Brown, looking calmly on the Northern Islander's struggle with the elements, tries to fathom God's purpose. Muir meantime regards his youth in Orkney as a blissful dawn and looks on city life with horror. Edwin Morgan, on the other hand, bred in Glasgow, loves the city while he is sensitively aware of its squalor and violence which he abhors. MacDiarmid, the dominant figure in the new Scottish movement, speaks for Scotland, lamenting its betrayal by and to the English, its neglect by its own people and its decadence, and declares its need for a new spirit. Simultaneously he is writing truly international poetry. Each of the twelve poets has an individual contribution to make.

The printing of texts of poems in Scots offers certain difficulties. Since the time of Burns, no system has been generally adopted for Scots orthography and punctuation and though this resulted in untidiness, there was no urgent need for uniformity while the general public spoke Scots. After a meeting of the Makars' Club in 1947 attended by many prominent Scottish poets the Scots Style Sheet, reproduced on page 17, was drawn up and many poets since then have adopted its proposals. It was felt that no good could come of normalising spelling or punctuation in the anthology and so no author's texts have been altered in any way.

In the anthology are a number of poems not previously published and for those I wish to express my thanks to the authors. Every living poet represented in this anthology has given me the benefit of his personal help and advice and for this privilege I am most deeply grateful.

The compilation of this critical anthology would have been for me impossible without the invaluable help from those friends and members of the English Association committee, given freely to me at all stages of the work: Mr George More, George Watson's College; Dr Ian Campbell, University of Edinburgh; Dr John Low, Moray House College of Education; Mr John Blackburn, Golspie High School and Miss Alison Foster, late of James Gillespie's High School.

To Dr Ian Campbell special thanks are due both for help throughout the project and for reading the final manuscript and suggesting valuable improvements. I am greatly indebted to Dr W. R. Aitken of Strathclyde University for help with the poetry of Soutar and with the bibliography, to Mrs Isobel Atkinson for her skill and patience in typing the manuscript, and to my colleague Mr J. K. Annand for expert advice on Scots and for frank criticism. I am deeply grateful to Professor John MacQueen for his help and counsel during the preparation of this work and for his kind preface to it.

Finally I value greatly the friendship and help of Mr Stanley Foster and his staff of the University of London Press in making this such a handsome volume.

CHARLES KING
Secretary, The English Association
Edinburgh Branch

Edinburgh, 1971

SCOTS STYLE SHEET

(As proposed at the Makars' Club meeting on 11th April 1947 in Edinburgh)
Reprinted from *Lines Review* No. 9, August 1955

Aa for older 'all' and colloquial 'a': caa, baa, smaa, faa, staa. But ava, awa, wha. And snaw, blaw, braw etc.

Ae, ai, ay, or *a* (consonant) *e* for the open sound in fray, frae, hain, cairt, maister, blae, hame, bane, byspale. Also *ay* for yes; *aye* for always.

E, ee, ei, ie and *i* for the sound of 'i' in French: according to old usage: heed, deed, heid, deid, hie, Hieland, die; Hevin, sevin, elevin; ee, een, yestreen; ambition, king, tradition, sanctified.

Eu for the sound in neuk, deuk, leugh, leukit, beuk, eneuch – pronounced variously from north to south and from east to west.

Ie for diminutive, adjectival and adverbial endings – mannie, bonnie and lichtlie.

Y for the diphthong 'a-i' in wynd, mynd, hyst in distinction to plain short 'i' in wind, bind, find. (The practice of dropping the terminal 'd' to be discouraged in writing.)

Ou mainly for sound of French *ou* in mou, mouth, south, sou, about, out, nou, hou, dour, douce, couthie, drouth, toun, doun, round; but *oo* according to old usage in words like smooth, smool, snoove.

Ow, owe always for the diphthong in powe, knowe, growe, thow, rowe, gowpit, yowl.

Ui or *u* (consonant) *e* for the modified 'u' sound, long and short, puir, muir, fluir; guid, tuim, wuid; spune, shune, sune, tune, use, mune, abune.

17

Ch guttural in all cases where this sound is to be represented, socht, bocht, thocht, eneuch, teuch; the obsolete 'gh' might profitably be dropped in 'through' and 'though' – throu, tho – and 'laigh' spelt 'laich'. But 'delyte', never rhyming with 'nicht'.

Verbal endings: -an for all present participles, but -in for the verbal noun in 'newbiggin', 'flytin', etc. Past tense and past participles of weak verbs in -it, -t and -ed according to euphony: flypit, skailt, garred, snawed, loued.

Ane for yin, een, etc. (one). Ae, not yae, before nouns. Ain for own, his ain sel, etc. But awn (wha's aucht) for 'own' (verb).

Pronouns: wha, interrog., nom. and accus.; and 'that' as relative in preference to 'wha' or 'whilk'. 'Whatna' rather than 'whilk' as interrogative adjective: Whatna ane was that?

To: use this spelling before infinitive, and 'til' as a rule before nouns – but euphony must be the guide. We gaed til the kirk.

Tae: too meaning also, and toe.

Negatives: -na affixed to verb, nae before noun, and no normally. I'm no that fou.

Edwin Muir

Born on a farm at Deerness in Orkney, in 1887, Muir received his education on the islands before moving to Glasgow where he worked for some years mainly as a clerk. He married Willa Anderson in 1919 in London where he took up literary work including book reviewing, an occupation which he continued to practise throughout his life. T. S. Eliot believed Muir's criticism to be among the best of our time. He wrote a considerable amount of other prose perhaps the best of which is *An Autobiography*. He and his wife translated a great deal, mainly from German, notably the works of Franz Kafka. He was appointed by the British Council to posts in Edinburgh, Rome and Prague, was awarded honorary degrees by many universities and in 1950 became the first Warden of Newbattle Abbey, Midlothian, a residential college for adult education. In 1954 he was appointed to the Charles Eliot Norton Professorship at Harvard University. After returning from the USA, he lived near Cambridge until his death in 1959. His first volume was *First Poems* in 1925 and further volumes appeared at irregular intervals until his *Collected Poems 1921-1958* was published in 1960.

When Muir left pastoral Orkney for industrial Glasgow where he s. w for the first time poverty, squalor, degradation and death, the move seemed, in retrospect, the Fall from an Eden of timeless innocence. These surface events of life, which he called 'The Story', appeared to reflect a meaningless chaos and when he and his wife translated Kafka's works, the poet at first shared the agonizing frustration and bewilderment of the characters therein. For years he strove to find some pattern by penetrating beneath the surface maze of life to a profounder significance – 'The Fable'. In *An Auto- biography* 1954, the best introduction to his poetry, he amplified the pattern of 'Eden and the Fall', first outlined in *The Story and the Fable* 1940 and applied it first to his own life and then to human life as a whole.

We see the maze of life in his poem 'The Labyrinth'. Anyone who reads aloud the first long sentence of 35 lines is bound to gain some feeling of the bewildering complex windings of meaningless living. But towards the end of the poem, there is a vision of human life as a meaningful part of a larger pattern

> . . . and this our life
> Was as a chord deep in that dialogue,
> As easy utterance of harmonious words,
> Spontaneous syllables bodying forth a world.

In a sense, much of Muir's poetry is 'syllables bodying forth a world', the world of his Fable, in which suffering and injustice are given a meaning and a place. This can be seen, for example in 'One Foot in Eden':

> But famished field and blackened tree
> Bear flowers in Eden never known.
> Blossoms of grief and charity
> Bloom in these darkened fields alone.
> What had Eden ever to say
> Of hope and faith and pity and love
> Until was buried all its day
> And memory found its treasure trove?
> Strange blessings never in Paradise
> Fall from these beclouded skies.

These two poems give some indication of how Muir's insight continued to develop. Eventually he found that the basic doctrines of Christianity harmonised with his fable and illuminated it, to make it yet more profound and all embracing.

From the secure standpoint of a deep coherent vision of life, he could write fine poetry on current topics such as the rape of Czechoslovakia in 1948 or Atomic War in 'The Good Town', 'The Horses', 'The Last War' and 'The Day Before the Last Day'. These poems throw light on our own times certainly but at the same time they have a universal significance and that is where their true greatness lies.

Because of Muir's outlook, symbolism is inevitable in his work, and this gives a richness and density to much of his poetry. The comparison with Wordsworth's attitude to childhood and early life is also inevitable and certainly valid. Like the older poet too, Muir aims at a deceptive simplicity of language and style untouched by stylistic innovation. His command of language and verse forms, however, deepened with his philosophy so that, like Yeats, he developed in power as a poet, the older he grew.

Childhood

Long time he lay upon the sunny hill,
  To his father's house below securely bound.
Far off the silent, changing sound was still,
  With the black islands lying thick around.

He saw each separate height, each vaguer hue,
  Where the massed islands rolled in mist away,
And though all ran together in his view
  He knew that unseen straits between them lay.

Often he wondered what new shores were there.
  In thought he saw the still light on the sand,
The shallow water clear in tranquil air,
  And walked through it in joy from strand to strand.

Over the sound a ship so slow would pass
  That in the black hill's gloom it seemed to lie.
The evening sound was smooth like sunken glass,
  And time seemed finished ere the ship passed by.

Grey tiny rocks slept round him where he lay,
  Moveless as they, more still as evening came,
The grasses threw straight shadows far away,
  And from the house his mother called his name.

from First Poems 1925

Horses

Those lumbering horses in the steady plough,
On the bare field – I wonder why, just now,
They seemed terrible, so wild and strange,
Like magic power on the stony grange.

Perhaps some childish hour has come again,
When I watched fearful, through the blackening rain,
Their hooves like pistons in an ancient mill
Move up and down, yet seem as standing still.

Their conquering hooves which trod the stubble down
Were ritual that turned the field to brown,
And their great hulks were seraphim of gold,
Or mute ecstatic monsters on the mould.

And oh the rapture, when, one furrow done,
They marched broad-breasted to the sinking sun!
The light flowed off their bossy sides in flakes;
The furrows rolled behind like struggling snakes.

But when at dusk with steaming nostrils home
They came, they seemed gigantic in the gloam,
And warm and glowing with mysterious fire
That lit their smouldering bodies in the mire.

Their eyes as brilliant and as wide as night
Gleamed with a cruel apocalyptic light.
Their manes the leaping ire of the wind
Lifted with rage invisible and blind.

Ah, now it fades! it fades! and I must pine
Again for that dread country crystalline,
Where the blank field and the still-standing tree
Were bright and fearful presences to me.

from First Poems 1925

The wayside station

Here at the wayside station, as many a morning,
I watch the smoke torn from the fumy engine
Crawling across the field in serpent sorrow.
Flat in the east, held down by stolid clouds,
The struggling day is born and shines already
On its warm hearth far off. Yet something here
Glimmers along the ground to show the seagulls
White on the furrows' black unturning waves.

But now the light has broadened.
I watch the farmstead on the little hill,
That seems to mutter: 'Here is day again'
Unwillingly. Now the sad cattle wake
In every byre and stall,
The ploughboy stirs in the loft, the farmer groans
And feels the day like a familiar ache
Deep in his body, though the house is dark.
The lovers part
Now in the bedroom where the pillows gleam
Great and mysterious as deep hills of snow,
An inaccessible land. The wood stands waiting
While the bright snare slips coil by coil around it,
Dark silver on every branch. The lonely stream
That rode through darkness leaps the gap of light,
In voice grown loud, and starts its winding journey
Through the day and time and war and history.

from The Narrow Place 1943

Scotland 1941

We were a tribe, a family, a people.
Wallace and Bruce guard now a painted field,
And all may read the folio of our fable,
Peruse the sword, the sceptre and the shield.
A simple sky roofed in that rustic day,
The busy corn-fields and the haunted holms,
The green road winding up the ferny brae.

But Knox and Melville clapped their preaching palms
And bundled all the harvesters away,
Hoodicrow Peden in the blighted corn
Hacked with his rusty beak the starving haulms.
Out of that desolation we were born.

Courage beyond the point and obdurate pride
Made us a nation, robbed us of a nation.
Defiance absolute and myriad-eyed
That could not pluck the palm plucked our damnation.
We with such courage and the bitter wit
To fell the ancient oak of loyalty,
And strip the peopled hill and the altar bare,
And crush the poet with an iron text,
How could we read our souls and learn to be?
Here a dull drove of faces harsh and vexed,
We watch our cities burning in their pit,
To salve our souls grinding dull lucre out,
We, fanatics of the frustrate and the half,
Who once set Purgatory Hill in doubt.
Now smoke and death and money everywhere,
Mean heirlooms of each fainter generation,
And mummied housegods in their musty niches,
Burns and Scott, sham bards of a sham nation,
And spiritual defeat wrapped warm in riches,
No pride but pride of pelf. Long since the young
Fought in great bloody battles to carve out
This towering pulpit of the Golden Calf,
Montrose, Mackail, Argyle, perverse and brave,
Twisted the stream, unhooped the ancestral hill.
Never had Dee or Don or Yarrow or Till
Huddled such thriftless honour in a grave.

Such wasted bravery idle as a song,
Such hard-won ill might prove Time's verdict wrong,
And melt to pity the annalist's iron tongue.

from The Narrow Place 1943

The little general

Early in spring the little General came
  Across the sound, bringing the island death,
And suddenly a place without a name,
  And like the pious ritual of a faith,

Hunter and quarry in the boundless trap,
  The white smoke curling from the silver gun,
The feather curling in the hunter's cap,
  And clouds of feathers floating in the sun,

While down the birds came in a deafening shower,
  Wing-hurricane, and the cattle fled in fear.
Up on the hill a remnant of a tower
  Had watched that single scene for many a year,

Weaving a wordless tale where all were gathered
  (Hunter and quarry and watcher and fabulous field),
A sylvan war half human and half feathered,
  Perennial emblem painted on the shield

Held up to cow a never-conquered land
Fast in the little General's fragile hand.

from The Narrow Place 1943

For Ann Scott-Moncrieff (1914-1943)

Dear Ann, wherever you are
Since you lately learnt to die,
You are this unsetting star
That shines unchanged in my eye;
So near, inaccessible,
Absent and present so much
Since out of the world you fell,
Fell from hearing and touch –
So near. But your mortal tongue
Used for immortal use,
The grace of a woman young,
The air of an early muse,
The wealth of the chambered brow
And soaring flight of your eyes:
These are no longer now.
Death has a princely prize.

You who were Ann much more
Than others are that or this,
Extravagant over the score
To be what only is,
Would you not still say now
What you once used to say
Of the great Why and How,
On that or the other day?
For though of your heritage
The minority here began,
Now you have come of age
And are entirely Ann.

Under the years' assaults,
In the storm of good and bad,
You too had the faults
That Emily Brontë had,
Ills of body and soul,
Of sinner and saint and all
Who strive to make themselves whole,
Smashed to bits by the Fall.
Yet 'the world is a pleasant place'
I can hear your voice repeat,
While the sun shone in your face *from*
Last summer in Princes Street.   *The Voyage 1946*

The labyrinth

Since I emerged that day from the labyrinth,
Dazed with the tall and echoing passages,
The swift recoils, so many I almost feared
I'd meet myself returning at some smooth corner,
Myself or my ghost, for all there was unreal
After the straw ceased rustling and the bull
Lay dead upon the straw and I remained,
Blood-splashed, if dead or alive I could not tell
In the twilight nothingness (I might have been
A spirit seeking his body through the roads
Of intricate Hades) – ever since I came out
To the world, the still fields swift with flowers, the trees
All bright blossom, the little green hills, the sea,
The sky and all in movement under it,
Shepherds and flocks and birds and the young and old,
(I stared in wonder at the young and the old,
For in the maze time had not been with me;
I had strayed, it seemed, past sun and season and change,
Past rest and motion, for I could not tell
At last if I moved or stayed; the maze itself
Revolved around me on its hidden axis
And swept me smoothly to its enemy,
The lovely world) – since I came out that day,
There have been times when I have heard my footsteps
Still echoing in the maze, and all the roads
That run through the noisy world, deceiving streets
That meet and part and meet, and rooms that open
Into each other – and never a final room –
Stairways and corridors and antechambers
That vacantly wait for some great audience,
The smooth sea-tracks that open and close again,
Tracks undiscoverable, indecipherable,
Paths on the earth and tunnels underground,
And bird-tracks in the air – all seemed a part
Of the great labyrinth. And then I'd stumble
In sudden blindness, hasten, almost run,
As if the maze itself were after me
And soon must catch me up. But taking thought,
I'd tell myself, 'You need not hurry. This
Is the firm good earth. All roads lie free before you.'
But my bad spirit would sneer, 'No, do not hurry.

No need to hurry. Haste and delay are equal
In this one world, for there's no exit, none,
No place to come to, and you'll end where you are,
Deep in the centre of the endless maze.'

I could not live if this were not illusion.
It is a world, perhaps; but there's another
For once in a dream or trance I saw the gods
Each sitting on the top of his mountain-isle,
While down below the little ships sailed by,
Toy multitudes swarmed in the harbours, shepherds drove
Their tiny flocks to the pastures, marriage feasts
Went on below, small birthdays and holidays,
Ploughing and harvesting and life and death,
And all permissible, all acceptable,
Clear and secure as in a limpid dream.
But they, the gods, as large and bright as clouds,
Conversed across the sounds in tranquil voices
High in the sky above the untroubled sea,
And their eternal dialogue was peace
Where all these things were woven, and this our life
Was as a chord deep in that dialogue,
As easy utterance of harmonious words,
Spontaneous syllables bodying forth a world.

That was the real world; I have touched it once,
And now shall know it always. But the lie,
The maze, the wild-wood waste of falsehood, roads
That run and run and never reach an end,
Embowered in error – I'd be prisoned there
But that my soul has birdwings to fly free.

Oh these deceits are strong almost as life.
Last night I dreamt I was in the labyrinth,
And woke far on. I did not know the place.

from The Labyrinth 1949

The combat

It was not meant for human eyes,
That combat on the shabby patch
Of clods and trampled turf that lies
Somewhere beneath the sodden skies
For eye of toad or adder to catch.

And having seen it I accuse
The crested animal in his pride,
Arrayed in all the royal hues
Which hide the claws he well can use
To tear the heart out of the side.

Body of leopard, eagle's head
And whetted beak, and lion's mane,
And frost-grey hedge of feathers spread
Behind – he seemed of all things bred.
I shall not see his like again.

As for his enemy there came in
A soft round beast as brown as clay;
All rent and patched his wretched skin;
A battered bag he might have been,
Some old used thing to throw away.

Yet he awaited face to face
The furious beast and the swift attack.
Soon over and done. That was no place
Or time for chivalry or for grace.
The fury had him on his back.

And two small paws like hands flew out
To right and left as the trees stood by.
One would have said beyond a doubt
That was the very end of the bout,
But that the creature would not die.

For ere the death-stroke he was gone,
Writhed, whirled, into his den,
Safe somehow there. The fight was done,
And he had lost who had all but won.
But oh his deadly fury then.

A while the place lay blank, forlorn,
Drowsing as in relief from pain.
The cricket chirped, the grating thorn
Stirred, and a little sound was born.
The champions took their posts again.

And all began. The stealthy paw
Slashed out and in. Could nothing save
These rags and tatters from the claw?
Nothing. And yet I never saw
A beast so helpless and so brave.

And now, while the trees stand watching, still
The unequal battle rages there.
The killing beast that cannot kill
Swells and swells in his fury till
You'd almost think it was despair.

from The Labyrinth 1949

The annunciation

The angel and the girl are met.
Earth was the only meeting place.
For the embodied never yet
Travelled beyond the shore of space.
The eternal spirits in freedom go.

See, they have come together, see,
While the destroying minutes flow,
Each reflects the other's face
Till heaven in hers and earth in his
Shine steady there. He's come to her
From far beyond the farthest star,
Feathered through time. Immediacy
Of strangest strangeness is the bliss
That from their limbs all movement takes.
Yet the increasing rapture brings
So great a wonder that it makes
Each feather tremble on his wings.

Outside the window footsteps fall
Into the ordinary day
And with the sun along the wall
Pursue their unreturning way.
Sound's perpetual roundabout
Rolls its numbered octaves out
And hoarsely grinds its battered tune.

But through the endless afternoon
These neither speak nor movement make,
But stare into their deepening trance
As if their gaze would never break.

from One Foot in Eden 1956

One foot in Eden

One foot in Eden still, I stand
And look across the other land.
The world's great day is growing late,
Yet strange these fields that we have planted
So long with crops of love and hate.
Time's handiworks by time are haunted,
And nothing now can separate
The corn and tares compactly grown.
The armorial weed in stillness bound
About the stalk; these are our own.
Evil and good stand thick around
In the fields of charity and sin
Where we shall lead our harvest in.

Yet still from Eden springs the root
As clean as on the starting day.

Time takes the foliage and the fruit
And burns the archetypal leaf
To shapes of terror and of grief
Scattered along the winter way.
But famished field and blackened tree
Bear flowers in Eden never known.
Blossoms of grief and charity
Bloom in these darkened fields alone.
What had Eden ever to say
Of hope and faith and pity and love
Until was buried all its day
And memory found its treasure trove?
Strange blessings never in Paradise
Fall from these beclouded skies.

from One Foot in Eden 1956

To Franz Kafka

If we, the proximate damned, presumptive blest,
Were called one day to some high consultation
With the authentic ones, the worst and best
Picked from all time, how mean would be our station.
Oh we could never bear the standing shame,
Equivocal ignominy of non-election;
We who will hardly answer to our name,
And on the road direct ignore direction.

But you, dear Franz, sad champion of the drab
And half, would watch the tell-tale shames drift in
(As if they were troves of treasure) not aloof,
But with a famishing passion quick to grab
Meaning, and read on all the leaves of sin
Eternity's secret script, the saving proof.

from One Foot in Eden 1956

Scotland's winter

Now the ice lays its smooth claws on the sill,
The sun looks from the hill
Helmed in his winter casket,
And sweeps his arctic sword across the sky.
The water at the mill
Sounds more hoarse and dull.
The miller's daughter walking by
With frozen fingers soldered to her basket
Seems to be knocking
Upon a hundred leagues of floor
With her light heels, and mocking
Percy and Douglas dead,
And Bruce on his burial bed,
Where he lies white as may
With wars and leprosy,
And all the kings before
This land was kingless,
And all the singers before
This land was songless,
This land that with its dead and living waits the Judgment Day.
But they, the powerless dead,
Listening can hear no more
Than a hard tapping on the sounding floor
A little overhead
Of common heels that do not know
Whence they come or where they go
And are content
With their poor frozen life and shallow banishment.

from One Foot in Eden 1956

The horses

Barely a twelve month after
The seven days war that put the world to sleep,
Late in the evening the strange horses came.
By then we had made our covenant with silence,
But in the first few days it was so still
We listened to our breathing and were afraid.
On the second day
The radios failed; we turned the knobs; no answer.
On the third day a warship passed us, heading north,
Dead bodies piled on the deck. On the sixth day
A plane plunged over us into the sea. Thereafter
Nothing. The radios dumb;
And still they stand in corners of our kitchens,
And stand, perhaps, turned on, in a million rooms
All over the world. But now if they should speak,
If on a sudden they should speak again,
We would not listen, we would not let it bring
That old bad world that swallowed its children quick
At one great gulp. We would not have it again.
Sometimes we think of the nations lying asleep,
Curled blindly in impenetrable sorrow,
And then the thought confounds us with its strangeness.

The tractors lie about our fields; at evening
They look like dank sea-monsters couched and waiting.
We leave them where they are and let them rust:
'They'll moulder away and be like other loam'.
We make our oxen drag our rusty ploughs,
Long laid aside. We have gone back
Far past our fathers' land.
                            And then, that evening
Late in the summer the strange horses came.
We heard a distant tapping on the road,
A deepening drumming; it stopped, went on again
And at the corner changed to hollow thunder.
We saw the heads
Like a wild wave charging and were afraid.
We had sold our horses in our father's time
To buy new tractors. Now they were strange to us
As fabulous steeds set on an ancient shield
Or illustrations in a book of knights.
We did not dare go near them. Yet they waited,

Stubborn and shy, as if they had been sent
By an old command to find our whereabouts
And that long-lost archaic companionship.
In the first moment we had never a thought
That they were creatures to be owned and used.
Among them were some half-a-dozen colts
Dropped in some wilderness of the broken world,
Yet new as if they had come from their own Eden.
Since then they have pulled our ploughs and borne our loads,
But that free servitude still can pierce our hearts.
Our life is changed; their coming our beginning.

from One Foot in Eden 1956

Hugh MacDiarmid

Christopher Murray Grieve, born in Langholm in 1892, considers his childhood in the Border country, with its historical associations, an important part of his intellectual history. He grew up an alert and intelligent youth, reading widely and enormously, aware of the Scottishness of his environment and of the complexity of the social and historical situation in the early part of this century in Scotland.

MacDiarmid's primary teacher at Langholm Academy, where he received most of his secondary education, was Francis George Scott, who later became the Scottish composer of songs *par excellence*. He set successfully to music a number of the MacDiarmid lyrics, and also certainly influenced the form of *A Drunk Man Looks at the Thistle*. His early career was in journalism, in various centres, and he became an energetic figure in literary circles partly as reviewer and writer, and suddenly a major poet in his own right. This happened with the rapid publication of three major books, *Sangschaw* 1925, *Penny Wheep* 1926 and *A Drunk Man Looks at the Thistle* 1926. At once, there was a growing awareness in Scotland that a major figure had emerged, capable of writing challenging verse in Scots, and in treating the contemporary Scottish scene in his poetry. In a century when prominent writers were turning increasingly to the use of English (Lewis Grassic Gibbon and Edwin Muir the outstanding examples) this had an electrifying effect on the Scottish literary scene, and many date the revival of writing in Scots in the present century to MacDiarmid's emergence in these three books. MacDiarmid himself was to turn increasingly to English for a medium of expression, a change of heart which to many marked the end of his good poetry, but this is to do an injustice to his later work, and the selection which appears in this anthology is designed to show the truly amazing range of his work.

The craftsmanship of the early poems, and the growing intellectual complexity of the later ones, is found in conjunction with a truly astonishing range of ideas and complexity of allusion. MacDiarmid's career, after his establishment as a major poet, was one of wordly failure along with literary success, and this led to prolonged unsettlement and diversification of energy. He spent years living in destitution in Shetland, working in a Clydeside shipyard or sailing in the Merchant Navy, and not until later in life was he financially secure. Continual change meant continual new experience, new ideas, new people. MacDiarmid has known very many outstanding personalities, and the extent of his knowledge is partly a result of his wide friendships (recorded in detail in *The Company I've kept* and *Lucky Poet*). It also arose from his restless desire for self-education and reading, and his reading in various languages and cultures has been enormous. All this leads to a poetry of diversity and complexity which offers an outstanding challenge to exegesis and criticism. MacDiarmid's is the poetry of ideas, particularly in his more recent work, and to overlook this fact is to do an injustice to his work in the manner of those who condemn him for leaving his early lyric mode for a more arid English poetry of ideas. The argument is that because the later poetry is frequently intellectual, English, non-lyric, it is bad. Patently this is wrong, for it is yet another instance of the diverse nature of MacDiarmid's work. For this reason this anthology reprints MacDiarmid's 'The Caledonian Antisyzygy' in which he explains, to some extent, the complexity of his own work,

> sometimes . . . the true lyric cry,
> Next but chopped-up prose.

MacDiarmid himself likens his diversity to the song of the nightingale, difficult to pin down either in character or in source. Its very elusiveness gives it its unique qualities, allows it to

> . . . find an emotion
> And vibrate in the memory as the song
> Of no other bird.

No poet of the present century has approached MacDiarmid's range of ideas, his mastery of lyric Scots, his universal appeal. More than anyone else in this anthology, MacDiarmid is a national poet with an international reputation.

The bonnie broukit bairn

Mars is braw in crammasy,
Venus in a green silk goun,
The auld mune shak's her gouden feathers,
Their starry talk's a wheen o' blethers,
Nane for thee a thochtie sparin',
Earth, thou bonnie broukit bairn!
– *But greet, an' in your tears ye'll droun*
The haill clanjamfrie!

from Sangschaw 1925

The watergaw

Ae weet forenicht i' the yow-trummle
I saw yon antrin thing,
A watergaw wi' its chitterin' licht
Ayont the on-ding;
An' I thocht o' the last wild look ye gied
Afore ye deed!

There was nae reek i' the laverock's hoose
That nicht – an' nane i' mine;
But I hae thocht o' that foolish licht
Ever sin' syne;
An' I think that mebbe at last I ken
What your look meant then.

from Sangschaw 1925

broukit streaked with tears, neglected   *braw* fine looking
crammasy crimson   *wheen o' blethers* a lot of nonsense
greet weep   *clanjamfrie* rabble
watergaw rainbow   *forenicht* evening
yow-trummle cold spell after time of sheep shearing
antrin rare   *chitterin'* shivering   *ayont* beyond
on-ding downpour   *gied* gave   *reek* smoke
laverock's hoose sky, firmament   *sin' syne* since then

Overinzievar

The pigs shoot up their gruntles here,
The hens staund hullerie,
And a' the hinds glower roond aboot
Wi' unco dullery.

Wi' sook-the-bluids and switchables
The grund's fair crottled up,
And owre't the forkit lichtnin' flees
Like a cleisher o' a whup!

from Sangschaw 1925

Crowdieknowe

Oh to be at Crowdieknowe
When the last trumpet blaws,
An' see the deid come loupin' owre
The auld grey wa's.

Muckle men wi' tousled beards,
I grat at as a bairn
'll scramble frae the croodit clay
Wi' feck o' swearin'.

An' glower at God an' a' his gang
O' angels i' the lift
— Thae trashy bleezin' French-like folk
Wha gar'd them shift!

Fain the weemun-folk'll seek
To mak' them haud their row
— *Fegs, God's no blate gin he stirs up*
The men o' Crowdieknowe!

from Sangschaw 1925

gruntles snouts	*hullerie* with feathers erect	*hinds* farm labourers
glower glare	*unco* great	*dullery* stupidity
sook-the-bluids little red beetles	*switchables* earwigs	*crottled* crumbled away
cleisher lash, crack	*loupin* leaping,	*wa's* walls
muckle big *croodit* crowded	*feck* a great deal	*lift* sky *gar'd* made
Fain anxious *haud their row* be quiet	*fegs* truly	*blate* afraid, scared

39

O Jesu Parvule

*Followis ane sang of the birth of Christ with
the tune of 'Baw lu la law'*
                              Godly Ballates

His mither sings to the bairnie Christ
Wi' the tune o' *Baw lu la law.*
The bonnie wee craturie lauchs in His crib
An' a' the starnies an' he are sib,
    Baw, baw, my loonikie, baw, balloo.

'Fa' owre ma hinny, fa' owre, fa' owre,
A'body's sleepin binna oorsels.'
She's drawn Him in tae the bool o' her breist
But the byspale's nae thocht o' sleep i' the least.
    Baloo, wee mannie, balloo, balloo.

from Sangschaw 1925

Wheesht, wheesht

Wheesht, wheesht, my foolish hert,
For weel ye ken
I widna ha'e ye stert
Auld ploys again.
It's guid to see her lie
Sae snod an' cool,
A' lust o' lovin' by –
Wheesht, wheesht, ye fule!

from Penny Wheep 1926

---

parvule (Latin), tiny   *craturie* creature   *starnies* stars
sib related   *hinny* honey   *fa' owre* drop off
binna except   *byspale* wee rascal
wheesht be quiet   *widna hae* would not have   *ploys* games
snod smooth, neat

Empty vessel

I met ayont the cairney
A lass wi' tousie hair
Singin' till a bairnie
That was nae langer there.

Wunds wi' warlds to swing
Dinna sing sae sweet,
The licht that bends owre a'thing
Is less ta'en up wi't.

from Penny Wheep 1926

Sic transit gloria Scotia

1   I amna' fou' sae muckle as tired – deid dune.
It's gey and hard wark coupin' gless for gless
Wi' Cruivie and Gilsanquhar and the like,
And I'm no' juist as bauld as aince I wes.

2   The elbuck fankles in the coorse o' time,
The sheckle's no' sae souple, and the thrapple
Grows deef and dour: nae langer up and doun
Gleg as a squirrel speils the Adam's apple.

3   Forbye, the stuffie's no' the real Mackay,
The sun's sel' aince, as sune as ye began it,
Riz in your vera saul: but what keeks in
Noo is in truth the vilest "saxpenny planet."

ayont beyond, on the other side of
cairney pile of stones used as marks   *a'thing* everything
muckle much   *dune* done, exhausted   *gey and* very
coupin' emptying   *bauld* bold   *elbuck* elbow
fankles becomes clumsy   *sheckle* wrist   *thrapple* windpipe
dour stubborn   *gleg* nimble   *speils* climbs
sun's sel the very sun   *riz* rose   *keeks* looks, peeps

4   And as the worth's gane doun the cost has risen.
      Yin canna thow the cockles o' yin's hert
      Wi'oot ha'en' cauld feet noo, jalousin' what
      The wife'll say (I dinna blame her fur't).

5   It's robbin' Peter to pey Paul at least . . .
      And a' that's Scotch aboot it is the name,
      Like a' thing else ca'd Scottish nooadays
      – A' destitute o' speerit juist the same.

6   (To prove my saul is Scots I maun begin
      Wi' what's still deemed Scots and the folk expect,
      And spire up syne by visible degrees
      To heichts whereo' the fules ha'e never recked.

7   But aince I get them there I'll whummle them
      And souse the craturs in the nether deeps,
      – For it's nae choice, and ony man s'ud wish
      To dree the goat's weird tae as weel's the sheep's!)

8   Heifetz in tartan, and Sir Harry Lauder!
      Whaur's Isadora Duncan dancin' noo?
      Is Mary Garden in Chicago still
      And Duncan Grant in Paris – and me fou'?

9   *Sic transit gloria Scotia* – a' the floo'ers
      O' the Forest are wede awa'. (A blin' bird's nest
      Is aiblins biggin' in the thistle tho'? . . .
      And better blin' if'ts brood is like the rest!)

10   You canna gang to a Burns supper even
      Wi'oot some wizened scrunt o' a knock-knee
      Chinee turns roon to say 'Him Haggis—velly goot!'
      And ten to wan the piper is a Cockney.

thow warm   *cauld* cold   *jalousin'* guessing
speerit spirit   *maun* must   *syne* after
fules fools   *whummle* overturn *s'ud* should
dree suffer   *weird* fate   *tae* also
Sic transit gloria Scotia Thus Scotland's glory passes
floo'ers flowers   *wede awa'* withered   *aiblins* possibly
biggin building   *scrunt* dwarf

11   No' wan in fifty kens a wurd Burns wrote
But misapplied is a'body's property,
And gin there was his like alive the day
They'd be the last a kennin' haund to gi'e –

12   Croose London Scotties wi' their braw shirt fronts
And a' their fancy freen's, rejoicin'
That similah gatherings in Timbuctoo,
Bagdad – and Hell, nae doot – are voicin'

13   Burns' sentiments o' universal love,
In pidgin' English or in wild-fowl Scots,
And toastin' ane wha's nocht to them but an
Excuse for faitherin' Genius wi' *their* thochts.

14   A' *they've* to say was aften said afore
A lad was born in Kyle to blaw aboot.
What unco fate mak's *him* the dumpin'-grun'
For a' the sloppy rubbish they jaw oot?

15   Mair nonsense has been uttered in his name
Than in ony's barrin' liberty and Christ.
If this keep spreedin' as the drink declines,
Syne turns to tea, wae's me for the *Zeitgeist!*

16   Rabbie, wad'st thou wert here – the warld hath need,
And Scotland mair sae, o' the likes o' thee!
The whisky that aince moved your lyre's become
A laxative for a' loquacity.

17   O gin they'd stegh their guts and haud their wheesht
I'd thole it, for 'a man's a man,' I ken,
But though the feck ha'e plenty o' the 'a' that,'
They're nocht but zoologically men.

18   I'm haverin', Rabbie, but ye understaun'
It gets my dander up to see your star
A bauble in Babel, banged like a saxpence
'Twixt Burbank's Baedeker and Bleistein's cigar.

a'body's anybody's	*gin* if	*kennin'* knowing, recognizing
croose conceited	*freends* friends	*unco* remarkable
wad'st would that	*stegh* stuff	
haud their wheesht remain silent	*thole* bear	*feck* majority
haverin' talking nonsense	*dander* temper	

19   There's nane sae ignorant but think they can
Expatiate on *you*, if on nae ither,
The sumphs ha'e ta'en you at your wurd, and, fegs!
The foziest o' them claims to be a – Brither!

20   Syne 'Here's the cheenge' – the star o' Rabbie Burns.
Sma' cheenge, 'Twinkle Twinkle.' The memory slips
As G. K. Chesterton heaves up to gi'e
'The Immortal Memory' in a huge eclipse,

21   Or somebody else as famous if less fat.
You left the like in Embro in a scunner
To booze wi' thieveless cronies sic as me.
I'se warrant you'd shy clear o' a' the hunner

22   Odd Burns Clubs tae, or ninety-nine o' them,
And haud your birthday in a different kip
Whaur your name isna ta'en in vain – as Christ
Gied a' Jerusalem's Pharisees the slip,

23   – Christ wha'd ha'e been Chief Rabbi gin he'd lik't! –
Wi' publicans and sinners to foregather,
But, losh! the publicans noo are Pharisees,
And I'm no' shair o' maist the sinners either.

24   But that's aside the point! I've got fair waun'ert.
It's no' that I'm sae fou' as juist deid dune,
And dinna ken as muckle's whar I am
Or hoo I've come to sprawl here 'neth the mune.

25   That's it! It isna me that's fou' at a',
But the fu' mune, the doited jade, that's led
Me fer agley, or 'mogrified the warld.
– For a' I ken I'm safe in my ain bed.

26   *Jean*! *Jean*! Gin she's no' here it's no' *oor* bed,
Or else I'm dreamin' deep and canna wauken,
But it's a fell queer dream if this is no'
A real hillside – and thae things thistles and bracken!

sumphs simpletons, fools	*fegs* truly	*foziest* softest
scunner disgust	*Embro* Edinburgh	
thieveless worthless, spiritless	*I'se* I should	*hunner* hundred
kip place *shair* sure	*waun'ert* wandered	*neth* beneath
doited crazed *agley* astray	*'mogrified* transformed, transmuted	

27   It's hard wark haud'n by a thocht worth ha'en'
And harder speakin't, and no' for ilka man;
Maist Thocht's like whisky – a thoosan' under proof,
And a sair price is pitten on't even than.

28   As Kirks wi' Christianity ha'e dune,
Burns' Clubs wi' Burns – wi' a' thing it's the same,
The core o' ocht is only for the few,
Scorned by the mony, thrang wi'ts empty name.

29   And a' the names in History mean nocht
To maist folk but 'ideas o' their ain',
The vera opposite o' onything
The Deid 'ud awn gin they cam' back again.

30   A greater Christ, a greater Burns, may come.
The maist they'll dae is to gi'e bigger pegs
To folly and conceit to hank their rubbish on.
They'll cheenge folks' talk but no' their natures, fegs!

from A Drunk Man Looks at the Thistle 1926

My quarrel with England

And let me pit in guid set terms
My quarrel wi' th'owre sonsy rose,
That roond about its devotees
A fair fat cast o' aureole throws
That blinds them, in its mirlygoes,
To the necessity o' foes.

haud'n holding   *ilka* every   *sair* ruinous   *pitten* put
ocht anything   *thrang* busy   *'ud* would   *awn* own   *hank* fasten
pit put   *owre* over   *sonsy* complacent   *mirlygoes* dazzle

Upon their King and system I
Glower as on things that whiles in pairt
I may admire (at least for them),
But wi' nae claim upon my hert,
While a' their pleasure and their pride
Ootside me lies – and there maun bide.

Ootside me lies – and mair than that,
For I stand still for forces which
Were subjugated to mak' way
For England's poo'er, and to enrich
The kinds o' English, and o' Scots,
The least congenial to my thoughts.

Hauf his soul a Scot maun use
Indulgin' in illusions,
And hauf in gettin' rid o' them
And comin' to conclusions
Wi' the demoralisin' dearth
O' onything worth while on Earth. . . .

from A Drunk Man Looks at the Thistle 1926

Of John Davidson*

I remember one death in my boyhood
That next to my father's, and darker, endures;
Not Queen Victoria's, but Davidson, yours,
And something in me has always stood
Since then looking down the sandslope
On your small black shape by the edge of the sea,
– A bullet-hole through a great scene's beauty,
God through the wrong end of a telescope.

from Scots Unbound and other Poems 1932

glower frown   *whiles* at times   *maun* must   *bide* remain

* Scottish Poet who committed suicide in 1909

On the ocean floor

Now more and more on my concern with the lifted
    waves of genius gaining
I am aware of the lightness depths that beneath them
    lie;
And as one who hears their tiny shells incessantly
    raining
On the ocean floor as the foraminifera die.

from Second Hymn to Lenin and other Poems 1935

After two thousand years

The Christians have had two thousand years
    And what have they done? –
Made the bloodiest and beastliest world ever seen
    Under the sun.

No Christian refuses to profit himself
    From his brother's misfortune.
The devil who would sup with our Christian banks
    Must sup with a hellish long spoon.

The Christian Churches are all built up
    In utter defiance of all Christ taught.
Co-religionists war at home and abroad,
    Each side supported by the self-same God.

And blandly the Bishops bestow their blessings
    On any murderer or fraud with the wit
To pay them, lip-serve the Cross, and keep
    The working-classes carrying it.

from Second Hymn to Lenin and other Poems 1935

The kind of poetry I want

A poetry the quality of which
Is a stand made against intellectual apathy,
Its material founded, like Gray's, on difficult knowledge,
And its metres those of a poet
Who has studied Pindar and Welsh poetry,
But, more than that, its words coming from a mind
Which has experienced the sifted layers on layers
Of human lives – aware of the innumerable dead
And the innumerable to-be-born,
The voice of the centuries, of Shakespeare's history plays
Concentrated and deepened,
'The breath and finer spirit of all knowledge,
The impassioned expression
Which is in the countenance of all science.'

A speech, a poetry, to bring to bear upon life
The concentrated strength of all our being
(Eloquent of victory in the stern struggle for self-conquest
– Real freedom; life free, unhampered, unalloyed;
A deep religious impulse moving us, not that
Interpreted by others through systems of belief and practice,
But the craving for the perfect synthesis of thought and action
Which alone can satisfy our test
Of ultimate truth, and conception of life's purpose.)
And not like only the 8 per cent of the fuel
That does useful work in the motor-car – the bare 2 per cent
The best incandescent lamp converts of the energy received
Into radiation visible to the human eye
– Against the glow-worm's 96 per cent efficiency.

Is not this what we require?
Coleridge's esemplasy and coadunation
Multeity in unity – not the Unity resulting
But the mode of the conspiration
(Schelling's *In-eins-bildung-kraft*)
Of the manifold to the one,
For, as Rilke says, the poet must know everything,
Be μινδεδνεος* (a phrase which I have borrowed
From a Greek monk, who applies it
To a Patriarch of Constantinople),

* myriad-minded

48

Or, as the Bhagavad-Gita puts it, *visvato-mukha*.*
A poetry full of erudition, expertise, and ecstasy
– The acrobatics and the faceted fly-like visions,
'Jacinth work of subtlest jewellery,' poetry *à quatre épingles* –
(Till above every line we might imagine
A tensely flexible and complex curve
Representing the modulation,
Emphasis, and changing tone and tempo
Of the voice in reading;
The curve varying from line to line
And the lines playing subtly against one another
– A fineness and profundity of organization
Which is the condition of a variety great enough
To express all the world's,
As subtle and complete and tight
As the integration of the thousands of brush strokes
In a Cézanne canvas),
Alive as a bout of all-in wrestling,
With countless illustrations like my photograph
        of a Mourning Dove
Taken at a speed of $1/75,000$ of a second.
A poetry that speaks 'of trees,
From the cedar tree that is in Lebanon
Even unto the hyssop that springeth out of the wall,'
And speaks also 'of beasts and of fowl,
And of creeping things and of fishes,'
And needs, like Marya Sklodowska on her laboratory tables,
For its open-eyed wonderment at the varied marvels of life,
Its insatiable curiosity about the mainspring,
Its appetite for the solution of problems,
Black fragments of pitch-blende from Saxony and Bohemia,
Greenish-blue chalcolite from Portugal and Tonkin.
Siskin-green uranium mica from France,
Canary-yellow veined carnotite from Utah,
Greenish-grey tjujamunite from Turkestan,
Pinkish-grey tjujamunite from Turkestan,
Pinkish-grey fergusonite from Norway,
Gold-tinted Australian monazite sand,
Greenish-black betafite from Madagascar,
And emerald-green tobernite from Indo-China.
And like my knowledge of, say, interlocking directorships,

* facing in all directions

Which goes far beyond such earlier landmarks
As the Pujo Committee's report
Or Louis Stanley's 'Spider Chart';
And everywhere without fear of Chestov's 'suddenly,'
Never afraid to leap, and with the unanticipatedly
Limber florescence of fireworks as they expand
Into trees or bouquets with the abandon of 'unbroke horses.'
Or like a Beethovian semitonal modulation to a wildly remote key,
As in the Allegretto where that happens with a sudden jump
    of seven sharps,
And feels like the sunrise gilding the peak of the Dent Blanche
While the Arolla valley is still in cloud.
And constantly with the sort of grey-eyed gaiety
So many people feel exalted by being allowed to hear
But are unable to laugh at – as in the case of the don
Who, lecturing on the First Epistle to the Corinthians
In a note on the uses of *αλλα* mentioned *αλλα precantis,*
Which an undergraduate took down as *Allah precantis*!

from Lucky Poet 1943

The Caledonian antisyzygy

I write now in English and now in Scots
To the despair of friends who plead
For consistency; sometimes achieve the true lyric cry,
Next but chopped-up prose; and write whiles
In traditional forms, next in a mixture of styles.
So divided against myself, they ask:
How can I stand (or they understand) indeed?

Fatal division in my thought they think
Who forget that although the thrush
Is more cheerful and constant, the lark
More continuous and celestial, and, after all,
The irritating cuckoo unique
In singing a true musical interval,
Yet the nightingale remains supreme,

The nightingale whose thin high call
And that deep throb,
Which seem to come from different birds
In different places, find an emotion
And vibrate in the memory as the song
Of no other bird – not even
The love-note of the curlew –
                    can do!

from Collected Poems 1962

Stony limits
In Memoriam: Charles Doughty, 1845-1926

Under no hanging heaven-rooted tree,
Though full of mammuks' nests,
Bone of old Britain we bury thee
But heeding your unspoken hests
Naught not coeval with the Earth
And indispensable till its end
With what whom you despised may deem the dearth
Of your last resting-place dare blend.
Where nature is content with little so are you
So be it the little to which all else is due.

Nor in vain mimicry of the powers
That lifted up the mountains shall we raise
A stone less of nature's shaping than of ours
    To mark the unfrequented place.
You were not filial to all else
Save to the Dust, the mother of all men,
And where you lie no other sign needs tell
(Unless a gaunt shape resembles you again
In some momentary effect of light on rock)
But your family likeness to all her stock.

Flowers may be strewn upon the grave
   Of easy come easy go.
Fitly only some earthquake or tidal wave
O'er you its red rose or its white may throw
But naught else smaller than darkness and light
– Both here, though of no man's bringing! –
And as any past time had been in your sight
Were you now from your bed upspringing,
Now or a billion years hence, you would see
Scant difference, eyed like eternity.

How should we have anything to give you
   In death who had nothing in life,
Attempting in our sand-riddles to sieve you
Who were with nothing but the sheer elements rife?
Anchor of truth, facile as granite you lie,
A plug suspended in England's false dreams.
Your worth will be seen by and by,
Like God's purpose in what men deem their schemes,
Nothing ephemeral can seek what lies in this ground
Since nothing can be sought but the found.

The poem that would praise you must be
Like the glass of some rock, sleek brown, crowded
With dark incipient crystal growths, we see;
Or a glimpse of Petavius may have endowed it
With the tubular and dumb-bell-shaped inclusions surrounded
   By the broad reaction rims it needs.
I have seen it in dreams and know how it abounded
– Ah! would I could find in me like seeds! –
As the north-easterly garden in the lunation grows,
A spectacle not one man in ten million knows.

I belong to a different country than yours
And none of my travels have been in the same lands
Save where Arzachel or Langrenus allures
Such spirits as ours, and the Straight Wall stands,
But crossing shear planes extruded in long lines of ridges
Torsion cylinders, crater rings, and circular seas
And ultra-basic xenoliths that make men look midges
Belong to my quarter as well, and with ease
I too can work in bright green and all the curious interference
Colours that under crossed nicols have a mottled appearance.

Let my first offering be these few pyroxenes twinned
On the orthopinacoid and hour-glass scheme,
Fine striae, microline cross-hatchings, and this wind
Blowing plumes of vapour forever it would seem
From cone after cone diminishing sterile and grey
In the distance; dun sands in ever-changing squalls;
Crush breccias and overthrusts; and such little array
Of Geology's favourite fal-de-lals
And demolitions and entrenchments of weather
As any turn of my eye brings together.

I know how on turning to noble hills
And stark deserts happily still preserved
For men whom no gregariousness fills
With the loneliness for which they are nerved
– The lonely at-one-ment with all worth while –
I can feel as if the landscape and I
Became each other and see my smile
In the corners of the vastest contours lie
And share the gladness and peace you knew,
– The supreme human serenity that was you!

I have seen Silence lift his head
And Song, like his double, lift yours,
And know, while nearly all that seems living is dead,
You were always consubstantial with all that endures,
Would it were on Earth! Not since Ezekiel has that faw sun ringed
A worthier head; red as Adam you stood
In the desert, the horizon with vultures black-winged,
And sang and died in this still greater solitude
Where I sit by your skull whose emptiness is worth
The sum of almost all the heads now on Earth
– By your roomy skull where most men might well spend
Longer than you did in Arabia, friend!

from Stony Limits and other Poems 1934

William Soutar

A Perth man (born 1898, died 1943), after war service in the Navy (1916-18) Soutar took a degree in English at Edinburgh University (1923). Already he had contracted a spinal illness which gradually overwhelmed him and confined him to bed for the last thirteen years of his short life. During this later period he published ten volumes of poems in Scots and English and wrote a diary (from which selections were published with the title *Diaries of a Dying Man*), a journal, and a large body of letters to friends and fellow writers.

Like MacDiarmid, whom he joined in the New Movement, he was anxious for the survival and strengthening of Scots and saw its best chance through bairn-rhymes ('If the Doric is to come back alive,' he wrote, 'it will come first on a cock-horse.') which appeared in *Seeds in the Wind* 1933. Two other volumes followed, *Poems in Scots* 1935 and *Riddles in Scots* 1937.

Soutar looked on the ballads, he called them 'the poems of Everyman', as the most haunting poetry in our language and himself produced a number worthy of our great tradition ('The Tryst' and 'Birthday' are fine examples). The ballad also influenced much of his other work. In his Whigmaleeries (fantastical poems), brief poems full of wit and delightful humour and all in Scots, Soutar is at his best. The great musician Orpheus is introduced as an orra-man playing the bagpipes and Will Todd returning home 'byordinar fou' has a friendly encounter with God.

Soutar avoids the mere whimsicality and quaintness of the Whistle-binkie School through fine sensitivity to language and a steady eye. Unlike many poets of the school of MacDiarmid, Soutar writes a pure Perthshire Scots. His verse has an essential singing quality. Many of his tender and happy songs for children such as 'The Gowk' and 'Day is Düne' have been set to music.

Although most of his best work is in Scots, Soutar could express himself seriously and profoundly in English, particularly on social and political themes. His pacifism burns particularly in 'The Guns', 'The Permanence of the Young Men', and 'The Unknown', while his distress for the suffering of innocent children in an air raid is nobly expressed in 'The Children'. One can also observe his perceptive sensibility in those poems inspired by Blake, for whom Soutar had a great admiration — 'In the Mood of Blake', and 'He Who Weeps for Beauty Gone'. The recurrence of the images in many poems of the Unicorn as a symbol of truth and Babylon as that of the Philistine world manifests Soutar's concern for the sins and folly of mankind.

Soutar is an accomplished artist. If he is prepared to use existing metrical patterns, he employs them with ingenuity and delicacy especially in his lyrics. In the comic and satirical poems, his dialogues, climaxes and rapier thrusts are deftly handled. His feeling for rhythm is most notable in the freer verse of 'The Return of the Swallow' and 'The Guns'. Through all his trials and sufferings, Soutar continued to concern himself with children and his fellow men. Determined to 'gang doun wi' a sang', he was still writing to within a day of his death,

Bed-time

Cuddle-doun, my bairnie;
The dargie day is düne:
Yon's a siller sternie
Ablow the siller müne.

Like a wabster body
Hingin on a threed,
Far abüne my laddie
And his wee creepie-bed.

from Collected Poems 1948

dargie busy   *siller* silver   *ablow* below
wabster spider   *abüne* above

Bawsy Broon

Dinna gang out the nicht:
Dinna gang out the nicht:
Laich was the müne as I cam owre the muir;
Laich was the lauchin though nane was there:
Somebody nippit me,
Somebody trippit me;
Somebody grippit me roun' and aroun':
I ken it was Bawsy Broon:
I'm shair it was Bawsy Broon.

Dinna win out the nicht:
Dinna win out the nicht:
A rottan reeshl'd as I ran be the sike,
And the dead-bell dunnl'd owre the auld kirk-dyke:
Somebody nippit me,
Somebody trippit me;
Somebody grippit me roun' and aroun':
I ken it was Bawsy Broon:
I'm shair it was Bawsy Broon.

from Seeds in the Wind 1933

Day is düne

Lully, lully, my ain wee dearie:
Lully, lully, my ain wee doo:
Sae far awa and peerieweerie
Is the hurlie o' the world noo.

And a' the noddin pows are weary;
And a' the fitterin feet come in:
Lully, lully, my ain wee dearie,
The darg is owre and the day is düne.

from Collected Poems 1948

Bawsy Broon brownie, hobgoblin		*dinna* don't	*gang* go
laich low	*lauchin* laughing	*shair* sure	*win* go
rottan rat	*reeshl'd* rustled	*sike* stream	*lully* softly
doo dove	*peerieweerie* tiny, minute	*hurlie* tumult	
fitterin pottering about			

The auld man o' Muckhart

The auld man o' Muckhart
Sae boo-backit is he
That whan he dovers owre
His neb is on his knee:

And whan he stechers oot
He gowks atween his legs:
'Hoch!' girns the auld man:
'It's grand for getherin eggs.'

'What'll ye dae, what'll ye dae,
Gin ye grow waur and waur?'
'Hoch!' yapps the auld man:
'I'll hae to gang on fower.'

'What'll ye dae, what'll ye dae,
Whan ye canna stap ava?'
'Hoch!' lauchs the auld man:
'I'll birl like a ba'.'

from Collected Poems 1948

boo-backit hump-backed
dovers falls into a slight slumber, dozes
neb nose   *stechers* staggers   *gowks* stares
girns grumbles   *gin* if   *waur* wors ·
fower all-fours   *ava* at all   *birl* spin

Samson

The hands that riv'd the lion's maw,
The hands that wi' nae sword nor spear
Brocht a hale army to the fa'
Like it had been a field o' bear,
Were hankl'd be a lassie's hair.

Samson, wha brak a raip like straw,
And dung the doors o' Ashkelon;
Wha heistit Gaza's gates awa,
Becam the byword o' the toun –
Afore he pu'd the pillars doun.

from Collected Poems 1948

Ae nicht at Amulree

Whan Little Dunnin' was a spree,
And no a name as noo,
Wull Todd wha wrocht at Amulree
Gaed hame byordinar fou.

The hairst had a' been gether'd in:
The nicht was snell but clear:
And owre the cantle o' the müne
God keekit here and there.

Whan God saw Wull he gien a lauch
And drappit lichtly doun;
Syne stüde ahint a frostit sauch
Or Wull cam styterin on.

fa' fall   *bear* barley   *hankl'd* entangled   *raip* rope
dung smashed   *heistit* lifted   *byword* laughing-stock
spree jollification   *wrocht* worked   *byordinar* exceptionally
hairst harvest   *snell* sharp   *cantle* crown, top   *styterin* staggering
keekit looked   *gien* gave   *ahint* behind   *sauch* willow

Straucht oot He breeng'd, and blared: 'Wull Todd!'
Blythe as Saint Johnstoun's bell:
'My God!' gowp'd Wull: 'Ye'r richt,' says God:
'I'm gled to meet yersel.'

from Collected Poems 1948

The tryst

O luely, luely cam she in
And luely she lay doun:
I kent her be her caller lips
And her breists sae sma' and roun'.

A' thru the nicht we spak nae word
Nor sinder'd bane frae bane:
A' thru the nicht I heard her hert
Gang soundin' wi' my ain.

It was about the waukrife hour
Whan cocks begin to craw
That she smool'd saftly thru the mirk
Afore the day wad daw.

Sae luely, luely, cam she in
Sae luely was she gaen
And wi' her a' my simmer days
Like they had never been.

from Poems in Scots 1935

breeng'd darted out suddenly
luely softly   *kent* knew   *caller* cool, fresh
sinder'd sundered, parted   *waukrife* sleepless
smool'd slipped away   *mirk* dark   *daw* dawn
gaen gone   *simmer* summer

Ballad

O! shairly ye hae seen my love
Doun whaur the waters wind:
He walks like ane wha fears nae man
And yet his e'en are kind.

O! shairly ye hae seen my love
At the turnin o' the tide;
For then he gethers in the nets
Doun be the waterside.

O! lassie I hae seen your love
At the turnin o' the tide;
And he was wi' the fisher-folk
Doun be the waterside.

The fisher-folk were at their trade
No far frae Walnut Grove;
They gether'd in their dreepin nets
And fund your ain true love.

from Collected Poems 1948

The children

Upon the street they lie
Beside the broken stone:
The blood of children stares from the broken stone.

Death came out of the sky
In the bright afternoon:
Darkness slanted over the bright afternoon.

whaur where   *wind* twist and turn   *dreepin* dripping
Walnut Grove a salmon fishing station on the Tay near Perth

Again the sky is clear
But upon earth a stain:
The earth is darkened with a darkening stain:

A wound which everywhere
Corrupts the hearts of men:
The blood of children corrupts the hearts of men.

Silence is in the air:
The stars move to their places:
Silent and serene the stars move to their places:

But from earth the children stare
With blind and fearful faces:
And our charity is in the children's faces.

from In the Time of Tyrants 1939

The guns

Now, on the moors where the guns bring down
The predestinated birds,
Shrill, wavering cries pass
Like the words of an international peace;
And I would that these cries were heard in every town,
Astounding the roar of the wheel
And the lying mouth of the news:
And I would that these cries might more and more increase
Until the machine stood still;
And men, despairing in the deathly queues,
Heard their own heart-beats
Shouting aloud, in the silence of the streets:
'Are we not also hand-fed in a wilderness:
What are we waiting for?'

from Collected Poems 1948

The permanence of the young men

No man outlives the grief of war
Though he outlive its wreck:
Upon the memory a scar
Through all his years will ache.

Hopes will revive when horrors cease;
And dreaming dread be stilled;
But there shall dwell within his peace
A sadness unannulled.

Upon his world shall hang a sign
Which summer cannot hide:
The permanence of the young men
Who are not by his side.

from The Expectant Silence 1944

The unknown

There is a shape of human kind
Still to be recognised;
A murdered man who haunts the mind
And is not exorcised.

From every battlefield he comes
In silent nakedness:
And he outlives the muffled drums,
The oblivion of grass.

He has no name; no seal of birth;
No sign of saint or slave:
He is a man of common earth
Born from a common grave.

Bone of our bone: blood of our blood:
Our freedom and our fate:
His sires raged in the savage wood,
And still his brothers hate.

His heritage is in his hands;
And in the light and air;
And in the earth whereon he stands;
For he is everywhere.

And yet he walks his native ground
An alien without rest,
Bearing Cain's curse and Abel's wound
Upon his flesh confessed:

Blood of our blood: bone of our bone:
Brother since time began:
Look on his anguish nor disown
That he is everyman.

from But the Earth Abideth 1943

In the mood of Blake

He who learns to love his wrath
Digs a pit in a blind-man's path:
He who slays a singing bird
Shall be deaf when the truth is heard:
He who hides his helping hand
Shall sow at last in the salt sand:
And he who laughs at his brother's tears
Shall meet the misery he fears.
Laughing children in the light
Heal the heart from its secret blight:
Singing children as they pass
Leave tenderness where a wound was.
When men bind armour on the breast
They crush the faith they have confessed:
But when they fear no brother's face
Truth walks about the market-place.

from Collected Poems 1948

The return of the swallow

We men who die
Feel the quick pulse of joy flood through the heart
When suddenly you dart
Across our sky.
Slowly the frail leaf, as a butterfly,
Breaks the imprisoning bud:
And, from the copse,
The cuckoo's parlance, in a singing sigh,
Slowly drops;
But you are swift;
And the flash of your wing on the eye
Startles the blood.
You are the moment of our entering
Into the spring:
Our leap from wintry barrenness to birth:
Our pledge from earth
That yet again we stand where we have stood.
O happy mood;
O happy, happy mood in which we are
Bodies that stare
As time's wing cleaves a wave-crest of life's flood.

from A Handful of Earth 1936

Birthday

There were three men o' Scotland
Wha rade intill the nicht
Wi' nae müne lifted owre their crouns
Nor onie stern for licht:

Nane but the herryin' houlet,
The broun mouse, and the taed,
Kent whan their horses clapper'd by
And whatna road they rade.

stern star   *houlet* owl   *taed* toad   *kent* knew   *whatna* which

Nae man spak to his brither,
Nor ruggit at the rein;
But drave straucht on owre burn and brae
Or half the nicht was gaen.

Nae man spak to his brither,
Nor lat his hand draw in;
But drave straucht on owre ford and fell
Or nicht was nearly düne.

There cam a flaucht o' levin
That brocht nae thunner ca'
But left ahint a lanely lowe
That wudna gang awa.

And richt afore the horsemen,
Whaur grumly nicht had been,
Stüde a' the Grampian Mountains
Wi' the dark howes atween.

Up craigie cleuch and corrie
They rade wi' stany soun',
And saftly thru the lichted mirk
The switherin' snaw cam doun.

They gaed by birk and rowan,
They gaed by pine and fir;
Aye on they gaed or nocht but snaw
And the roch whin was there.

Nae man brac'd back the bridle
Yet ilka fit stüde still
As thru the flichterin' floichan-drift
A beast cam doun the hill.

---

ruggit pulled, tugged   *straucht* straight
burn stream   *brae* hill   *gaen* gone
flaucht o' levin flash of lightning   *ca'* peal
ahint behind   *lowe* glow   *gang* go   *grumly* grim
howes hollows   *cleuch* glen, ravine   *mirk* dark
switherin' flurrying   *birk* birch   *roch* rough
ilka every   *fit* foot   *floichan-drift* snowflakes

It steppit like a stallion,
Wha's heid hauds up a horn,
And weel the men o' Scotland kent
It was the unicorn.

It steppit like a stallion,
Snaw-white and siller-bricht,
And on its back there was a bairn
Wha low'd in his ain licht.

And baith gaed by richt glegly
As day was at the daw;
And glisterin' owre hicht and howe
They saftly smool'd awa.

Nae man but socht his brither
And look't him in the e'en,
And sware that he wud gang a' gates
To cry what he had seen.

There were three men o' Scotland
A' frazit and forforn;
But on the Grampian Mountains
They saw the unicorn.

from Poems in Scots 1935

hauds holds   *low'd* glowed
gaed went   *richt* very   *glegly* quickly
hicht height   *smool'd* slipped
a' gates in every direction   *frazit* astonished
forforn worn out

Sang

Hairst the licht o' the müne
To mak a siller goun;
And the gowdan licht o' the sün
To mak a pair o' shoon:

Gether the draps o' dew
To hing about your throat;
And the wab o' the watergaw
To wark yoursel' a coat:

And you will ride oniewhaur
Upon the back o' the wind;
And gang through the open door
In the wa' at the world's end.

from Poems in Scots and English 1961

To the future

He, the unborn, shall bring
From blood and brain
Songs that a child can sing
And common men:

Songs that the heart can share
And understand;
Simple as berries are
Within the hand:

Such a sure simpleness
As strength may have;
Sunlight upon the grass:
The curve of the wave.

from The Expectant Silence 1944

hairst harvest	*gowdan* golden	*shoon* shoes
watergaw rainbow	*wark* make	
oniewhaur anywhere	*wa'* wall	

George Bruce

George Bruce was born in Fraserburgh in 1909 and his early life was influenced by the rocky sea-girt landscapes, and by the ways of the fishermen, the herring curers and others in the fishing industry who moved in his family circle. He was educated at Aberdeen University where he took an honours degree in English. After teaching for a time in Dundee, he was appointed a Programme Assistant with the B B C. Latterly he was Documentary Talks Producer in Edinburgh but retired in 1970 and is now engaged in full-time freelance writing. George Bruce for many years had a very influential position at the B B C, having produced for and worked with most of the leading Scottish creative artists of the day. As the power behind 'Scottish Life and Letters', a B B C Arts programme, he was concerned in keeping the Scottish people informed on all the arts. At Edinburgh Festival time, he became the intimate friend of a wide range of international performers. Appropriately enough, he is working on a critical historical account of twenty-five *Edinburgh Festivals*.

Bruce's poems reflect his abiding interest in the lives of the people of the North-east of Scotland and in the hard unyielding environment – the storm-swept shores, the rocks, the sea. The sense of place is deeply embedded in his work; and he sees in the fisherman's life an epitome of the plight of man. Complementary to this are his interest in and appreciation of foreign scenes and works of art – particularly Italian scenes and art. Painting and sculpture have had a strong appeal for him: his poetic technique is clearly influenced by the impact of these arts on his sensibility. His lyricism is restrained in its musical effects; and critics have written of the bareness and the athleticism of a poetic style that succeeds in transmitting a sense of the precariousness of life, a sympathy for the individual, a concern for mankind. Some of the best work comes as a result of seeing the universality and compassion behind great art – whether it be painting, sculpture or architecture. Of late a new ironic note has entered Bruce's work. Technically he admits to being influenced by T. S. Eliot, W. B. Yeats and particularly Ezra Pound; but the North-east Scots colouring, his austere Scottish 'music', and the bright hardness of his imagery bring out original and individual qualities.

Perhaps with his release from official position, his natural caution may be relaxed and a new side of his poetry emerge.

As this collection goes to press, George Bruce takes up an appointment as Creative Writing Fellow at the University of Glasgow.

Inheritance

This which I write now
Was written years ago
Before my birth
In the features of my father.

It was stamped
In the rock formations
West of my home town.
Not I write,

But, perhaps, William Bruce,
Cooper.
Perhaps here his hand
Well articled in his trade.

Then though my words
Hit out
An ebullition from
City or flower,

There not my faith,
These the paint
Smeared upon
The inarticulate,

The salt crusted sea-boot,
The red-eyed mackerel,
The plate shining with herring,
And many men,

Seamen and craftsmen and curers,
And behind them
The protest of hundreds of years,
The sea obstinate against the land.

from Selected Poems 1947

A child crying

The miserable moment
Breaks in your eyes
Breaks world, time, life in cries,
Spills all hope and pleasure upon the floor,
Tashes your body with the sore.

Fling a sunbeam in your eyes,
And frustrate every emblem of despair,
Cries to laughter, cries, cries, now laughter
Catch all morning air,
All sourness meadowfair.

from Sea Talk 1944

Homage to El Greco
The Agony in the Garden

Distant an unimportant soldiery,
(Those proscribed from bliss and agony
Living in worlds of space and time)
Sleepers, the garden of Gethsemane,
Depiction of His eyes and hands.

Look there in the garden
Where all shapes taken from
Hexagonal basalt to eruptive flame,
Prelude to the pattern
Of field and stream,
Retain, gather disruption,
Collect the flux of time and flame

To precipitate upon
The eyes that seek,
The hands that ask
The peace, the peace
Within the eyes that plead
The hands that speak,
Within the balls
The way, the life, the peace.

from Sea Talk 1944

The curtain

Half way up the stairs
Is the tall curtain.
We noticed it there
After the unfinished tale.

My father came home,
His clothes sea-wet,
His breath cold.
He said a boat had gone.

He held a lantern.
The mist moved in,
Rested on the stone step
And hung above the floor.

I remembered
The blue glint
Of the herring scales
Fixed in the mat,

And also a foolish crab
That held his own pincers fast.
We called him
Old Iron-clad.

I smelt again
The kippers cooked in oak ash.
That helped me to forget
The tall curtain.

from Selected Poems 1947

Death mask of a fisherman

My dead father speaks to me
In a look he wore when dying.
The emaciated hands and limbs
Pass from the memory.
But that mask appropriate to that moment
When he balanced between two worlds
Remains to rise again and again
Like an unanswered question.

He was going very fast then
To be distributed amongst the things
And creatures of the ground and sea.
He was ready for the shells and worms,
(Outside the rain stormed
And the small boats at the pier jolted)
His eyes had passed to the other side
Of terror and pain.

Night had settled in each.
The dissipation of feature,
The manifestation of skull,
The lengthening of cheek,
The dark filtering into the hollows,
Told *one* thing:
What speed towards our mother!

But another image here too,
Something I had seen before
Caverned in the El Greco face,
Something presented to us
From the other side of dream;
Translatable only in hints from the breathless world.

from Selected Poems 1947

A gateway to the sea
At the East Port, St Andrews

Pause stranger at the porch: nothing beyond
This framing arch of stone, but scattered rocks
And sea and these on the low beach
Original to the cataclysm and the dark.

Once one man bent to the stone, another
Dropped the measuring line, a third and fourth
Together lifted and positioned the dressed stone
Making wall and arch; yet others
Settled the iron doors on squawking hinge
To shut without the querulous seas and men.
Order and virtue and love (they say)
Dwelt in the town – but that was long ago.
Then the strangers at the gate, the merchants,
Missioners, the blind beggar with the dog,
The miscellaneous vendors (duly inspected)
Were welcome within the wall that held from sight
The water's brawl. All that was long ago.
Now the iron doors are down to dust,
But the stumps of hinge remain. The arch
Opens to the element – the stones dented
And stained to green and purple and rust.

Pigeons settle on the top. Stranger,
On this winter afternoon pause at the porch,
For the dark land beyond stretches
To the unapproachable element; bright
As night falls and with the allurement of peace,
Concealing under the bland feature, possession.
Not all the agitations of the world.

Articulate the ultimate question as do those waters
Confining the memorable and the forgotten;
Relics, records, furtive occasions – Caesar's politics
And he who was drunk last night:
Rings, diamants, snuff boxes, warships,
Also the less worthy garments of worthy men.
Prefer then this handled stone, now ruined
While the sea mists wind about the arch.
The afternoon dwindles, night concludes,
The stone is damp unyielding to the touch,
But crumbling in the strain and stress
Of the years: the years winding about the arch,
Settling in the holes and crevices, moulding
The dressed stone. Once one man bent to it,
Another dropped the measuring line, a third
And fourth positioned to make wall and arch
Theirs. Pause stranger at this small town's edge –
The European sun knew these streets
O Jesu parvule; Christus Victus, Christus Victor,
The bells singing from their towers, the waters
Whispering to the waters, the air tolling
To the air – the faith, the faith, the faith.

All this was long ago. The lights
Are out, the town is sunk in sleep.
The boats are rocking at the pier,
The vague winds beat about the streets –
Choir and altar and chancel are gone.
Under the touch the guardian stone remains
Holding memory, reproving desire, securing hope
In the stop of water, in the lull of night
Before dawn kindles a new day.

from Landscapes and Figures 1967

Late springs this North

Late springs this North and Spring
Is cold with sea-borne air.
Wind bursts in the wide country.
By dyke and ditch the whins flare
Hares leap in the new ploughed furrs
Folk gang at the business that's theirs.

Andra and Jockie
Scutter wi the tractor
Jean's i the kitchie
Dod's i the byre
Fred the orra loon
Chops kindlin for the fire.

Late springs this North, hard the sun,
Caller the wind that blows to the bone

from Landscapes and Figures 1967

The town

Between the flat land of the plain
And the brief rock – the town.
This morning the eye receives
(As if the space had not intervened,
As if white light of extraordinary transparency
Had conveyed it silent and with smooth vigour)
The granite edge, edifice of stone –
The new tenement takes the sun.
The shop fronts stare,
The church spire signals heaven,
The blue-tarred streets divide and open sea-ward,
The air leaps like an animal.

scutter work awkwardly   *orra loon* odd job boy
caller bracing

Did once the sea engulf all here and then
At second thought withdraw to leave
A sea-washed town?

from Sea Talk 1944

Visit in winter

In the Highland hotel
the highland waiter
is waxed: in the off-season
when stags rut and their roaring
quivers the icicles from the eaves,
inside, in a ten foot tall bell jar,
in rubbed morning coat,
napkin at the ready,
his brown eyes staring from his yellow
smooth skin, – preserved, deferential,
he stands waiting in his improbable world

for the incredible August people
who kill birds and deer –
and not for need.
At least he can be verified,
visible in a tall bell jar.
Of the rest who found significance
in killing birds and deer,
we only heard tell.

from Collected Poems 1970

Laötian Peasant Shot
seen on television war report documentary

He ran in the living air,
exultation in his heels.

A gust of wind will erect
a twisting tower of dried leaves
that will collapse when
the breath is withdrawn.

He turned momentarily,
his eyes looking into his fear,
seeking himself.

When he fell the dust
hung in the air
like an empty container
of him.

from Landscape and Figures 1967

Robert Garioch

Thae twa-three chuckie-stanes
I lay on Scotland's cairn
biggit by men of bigger banes
afore I was a bairn.

and men of greater micht
will trauchle up the brae
and lay abuin them on the hicht
mair wechty stanes nor thae.

This dedication to his 1949 collection of poems displays, with typical modesty, the aims of a superb but underrated poetic craftsman. Born in Edinburgh in 1909 and educated at the Royal High School, Robert Garioch took an Honours degree in English at Edinburgh University and, as was inevitable in the early 1930s for most Arts graduates, entered the teaching profession. In this he remained, except for war service, until his retiral in 1967 when he became a full-time writer. Garioch has long been recognized by his fellow Scottish poets for the fine artist he is. Until 1966, his poetry apart from the familiar 'Embro to the Ploy', was generally known only to a discerning few, but wider recognition came with the appearance of *Selected Poems* 1966.

Robert Garioch, first and foremost a satirist, following in the direct line of Fergusson and Burns, is a traditionalist in an age of violent change. Garioch assumes the persona of the ordinary working-man speaking an amalgam of classical Scots and the language of the street corner. His main targets are pomposity, insincerity and corruption in public life and the Church, bureaucracy, and the hard lot of the creative artist forced to teach or take up an unrewarding and disagreeable routine occupation.

As well as translating the plays of George Buchanan, Garioch, a fellow teacher in a small way of doing, has translated into racy

Scots the first of Buchanan's Latin Elegies, 'The Humanists' Trauchles in Paris', an early poem in which Buchanan draws a vivid picture of the Paris don with long hours, wretched remuneration and dull pupils, the teacher bearing his text in one hand and his tawse in the other. Garioch employs the eight-line traditional Scots stanza with lively language appropriate to the theme. In 'Garioch's repone (reply) til George Buchanan' he adopts the genially familiar epistolary manner, shortening his verses by one line, thus giving more force to his amply justified complaint of a twentieth-century schoolmaster. He is again genial in tone when he takes himself down for airs and graces in the sonnet, 'Did Ye See Me?'. After eight pompous rhymes in the octet, the tone changes and for the final punch line, he employs ten low words. There is a harsher note in 'Elegy' as he recalls two martinet headmasters under whom it was his ill-luck to serve. In 'Sisyphus' the choice of that legend to describe the dominie's daily darg is remarkably apt with the long 'bumpity' classical hexameter lines and mixture of Scots, slang and modern expressions such as tea-breaks, slipped discs and pay cheque. The sustained metaphor never falls flat and Garioch's pawky humour pervades the poem.

Robert Garioch's satire is particularly telling when he works within the narrow limits of the sonnet, no other Scottish poet ever having exploited this medium more effectively for the castigation of the fashion, folly and fraud of his times. He has produced two series, *Sax Roman Sonnets* (translated from Belli 1791-1863) and *Saxteen Edinburgh Sonnets*. The *Roman Sonnets* are much more than mere translations. Belli was a faithful Catholic but anti-clerical poet and his criticism of malpractices and lack of enthusiasm in the Church of *his* day are apt material for the genius of Garioch at his most powerful. Nothing since 'Holy Willie's Prayer' has the savagery of 'A Suggested Ceremony' in which the poet proposes some sacrifice of the hierarchy to revitalise the Church.

The *Saxteen Edinburgh Sonnets* range widely over events and personalities in 'Oddanbeery' as Garioch names his native city, borrowing an invention of Sydney Goodsir Smith. 'The seenil City Faithers' who 'hirple in borrowed tiles, fu' sanctimonious' to the Festival Opening Service in St Giles', the 'three choice notorious bailies' with the 'weill-kent heid yin' wining and dining at the City's expense, 'the cognoscenti' listening eidently to a tape-recording of 'Kurt Schwitters' Ur-Sonata' are all fair game for

Garioch. Although he is unsparing in his attacks, Robert Garioch never descends to the personal nor the partisan. Thus the satire can have a universality and timelessness that will ensure it a lasting place in literature.

If Garioch is at home with the sonnet, he is almost equally fluent in the fable where his kinship with Henryson is apparent. 'The Twa Mice' is a comparatively slight work but the handling of the subject is deft with not a word being wasted. In 'The Canny Hen', a more extensive poem, with the kind of social criticism found in Henryson, Garioch pokes fun at the new-fangled scientific approach to nutrition and the battery system of egg production. Here there are delightful echoes of Barbour and Burns.

Garioch's output although largely satirical in tone, includes war poems inspired by his experiences in the Desert and in Italy, a number of poems on historical subjects ('A Whig View of the '45 Rebellion' being one) and some quiet lyrics. Two of his most telling poems are 'To Robert Fergusson' and the sonnet 'At Robert Fergusson's Grave'. In the former poem he recalls the Edinburgh of 1770,

> . . . whan Embro was a quean
> sae weill worth seein,

wishing the two Roberts could have met and regrets the many novelties in the city today. The poem is charged with delightful historical reminiscence. In the sonnet however, Garioch is deadly serious and reverent of Scotland's literary tradition. No mocking here!

> . . . strang, present dool
> ruggs at my hairt. Lichtlie this gin ye daur:
> here Robert Burns knelt and kissed the mool.

As a craftsman, Robert Garioch is unsurpassed in modern Scottish poetry. His unerring sense of decorum, his feeling for rhythm, his brilliant handling of a variety of verse forms, all give his work true style. There is no more enjoyable a poet writing in Scotland today.

Garioch's repone till George Buchanan

Aye, George Buchanan, ye did weill
to wuss thae callants to the Deil
and lowse yoursel frae sic a creel;
    I've felt the same mysel.
We hearit your sad story throu
wi muckle sympathy, sae nou
    hear what I hae to tell.
I've screivit monie a sang and sonnet
sin owre my heid they waved thon bonnet
    made out of your auld breeks,
and see me nou, a makar beld
wi bleerit een and feet unstell'd
    no worth a cog of leeks.
And, like a leek upturned, I'm seen
white on the tap, but gey green
    in ither weys, I dout:
Maister of Arts, but wantan craft,
sma wunner some folk think I'm daft
    and snicker in their snout
to see me thole, week eftir week,
thon wey of life made ye that seik
ye utter'd thanks in Latin speik
    the day whan ye wan out.
A dominie wi darnit sark,
raxan his harns frae daw til dark,
    maun luik gey like a fule;
whan couthie dunces pey him hauf
of what he'd mak on onie staff
    outside a council schule.
Guid luck to ye! But as for me,
it's a life-sentence I maun dree,
the anelie chance of winning free
    that I may mention
wi houpe, sae faur as I can see,
    my teacher's pension.

repone reply	*wuss* wish	*callants* rascals
lowse free	*creel* basket	*screivit* scribbled
beld bald	*unstell'd* unsteady	*cog* bowl
gey very	*thole* bear	*wan out* escaped
sark shirt	*raxan* stretching	*harns* brains *maun* must
couthie prosperous	*dree* bear	

In kep and goun, the new M.A.,
wi burnisht harns in bricht array
    frae aa the bukes he's read,
nou realises wi dismay
he's left it owre late in the day
    to learn anither tred.
What has he got that he can sell?
nae maitter tho he scrieve a fell
guid-gauan prose style, Ethel M. Dell
    he canna rival.
Poetic pouers may win him praise
but guarantee nae fowth of days
    for his survival.
A kep and goun – what dae they maitter?
A kep and bells wad suit him better.
He's jist an orra human cratur,
    yaup as a lous.
Tho he be latinate and greekit,
he kens that ilka yett is steekit
    but Moray Hous.
Nou see him in his college blazer;
the Muse luiks on: it maun amaze her
    to see his tricks.
like shandy in the Galloway Mazer
or Occam tyauvan wi his razor
    to chop-up sticks.
Afore his cless he staunds and talks
or scrieves awa wi colour'd chalks;
nae mair by Helicon he walks,
    or e'en St Bernard's Well.
In clouds of blackbrod stour he's jowan
anent some aibstract plural noun,
while aa the time his hert is lowan
    in its wee private hell.
At nine a.m. she hears him blaw
his whustle, and lay doun the law
out in the pleygrund, whether snaw
    shoures doun, or Phoebus shines.
Wi muckle tyauve she sees him caa
chaos til order; raw by raw
he drills his bairns in mainner braw,

tred trade	*fell* very	*guid-gauan* fluent	*fowth* plenty
orra odd	*yaup* hungry	*tyauvan* struggling	*stour* dust
jowan talking	*anent* about	*lowan* burning *tyauve* effort	*braw* fine

weill covert-aff in lines.
They mairch til the assembly-haa
to sing a psalm and hear a saw
or maybe jist a threit or twa,
 as the heidmaister chuse.
Syne in his room she sees him faa
to wark; she hears him rant and jaw
and hoast and hawk and hum and haw,
blatter and blawp and bumm and blaw
and natter like a doitit craw,
teachan his bairns to count and draw
and chant gizinties and Bee-baw,
and read and spell and aa and aa,
faur owre taen-up wi maitters smaa
 to mind him of the Muse.
Whan schule has skailt, he maun awa,
whaur? ye may speir – to some green shaw
to meditate a poem? – Na!
His lowsan-time is faur
aheid: to organize fi'baw
 and plouter in the glaur.
Late in the day he hirples hame
wi bizzan heid, a wee-thing lame,
and indisjeesters in his wame,
 and that may cause nae wunner:
whan ither folk may dine at hame,
 he's dishan-out schule-denner.
Sae ilka week and month and year
his life is tined in endless steir,
grindan awa in second-gear
 gin teaching be his fate.
The Muse, wha doesna share her rule
wi sordid maisters, leaves the fule,
 sans merci, til his fate.

MORAL

Lat onie young poetic chiel
that reads thae lines tak tent richt weill:
THINK TWICE, OR IT'S OWRE LATE!

from
Selected
Poems
1966

threit threat	*hoast and hawk* cough	*natter* chatter	*doitit* silly
faurowre far too much	*skailt* emptied	*speir* ask	*lowsan* finishing
plouter flounder	*glaur* mud	*hirples* limps	*wame* belly
tined lost	*steir* struggle	*gin* if	*chiel* fellow	*or* before

Did ye see me?

I'll tell ye of ane great occasioun:
I tuke part in a graund receptioun.
Ye cannae hae the least perceptioun
hou pleased I wes to get the invitatioun

tae assist at ane dedicatioun.
And richtlie sae; frae its inceptioun
the hale ploy was my ain conceptioun;
I was asked to gie a dissertatioun.

The functioun was held in the aipen air,
a peety, that; the keelies of the toun,
a toozie lot, gat word of the affair.

We cudnae stop it; they jist gaithert roun
to mak sarcastic cracks and grin and stare.
I wisht I hadnae worn my M.A. goun.

from Selected Poems 1966

And they were richt

I went to see 'Ane Tryall of Hereticks'
by Fionn MacColla, treatit as a play;
a wycelike wark, but what I want to say
is mair taen-up wi halie politics

nor wi the piece itsel; the kinna tricks
the unco-guid get up til whan they hae
their wey. Yon late-nicht ploy on Setturday
was thrang wi Protestants and Catholics,

aipen open	*keelies* toughs	*toozie* rough
wycelike well-wrought	*halie* holy	*nor* than
kinna kind of	*ploy* entertainment	*thrang* crowded

an eydent audience, wi fowth of bricht
arguments wad hae kept them gaun til Monday.
It seemed discussion wad last out the nicht,
hadna the poliss, sent by Mrs Grundy
pitten us out at twelve. And they were richt!
Wha daur debait religion on a Sunday?

from Selected Poems 1966

Festival, 1962

The Festival sterts in a bleeze of gloir
wi sad processioun outbye St Giles':
Scotland's Estaiblishment in seemly files
wi siller trumpets sounan at the door.

The seenil City Faithers, that decoir
our seignories, hirple in borrowed tiles,
fu sanctimonious, til historic aisles
whaur Knox held furth and Jenny Geddes swore.

Sibilant crowds hiss, Thon yin's Shostakovich –
pointing admiringly wi mistaen finger –
Tadeucz Wronski, Oistrakh, Rostropovich.

Loud-speakers, gey distortit, gae their dinger;
some pacing provost – Thon yin's Aronowitz –
passes, to music frae *Die Meistersinger.*

from Selected Poems 1966

eydent keen   fowth plenty   gaun going
pitten put
sad sober   seenil rarely excellent   decoir adorn
seignories supreme courts   hirple limp
gae their dinger do their stuff

85

At Robert Fergusson's grave
October 1962

Canogait kirkyaird in the failing year
is auld and grey, the wee roseirs are bare,
five gulls leam white agen the dirty air:
why are they here? There's naething for them here.

Why are we here oursels? We gaither near
the grave. Fergussons mainly, quite a fair
turn-out, respectfu, ill at ease, we stare
at daith – there's an address – I canna hear.

Aweill, we staund bareheidit in the haar,
murnin a man that gaed back til the pool
twa-hunner year afore our time. The glaur

that haps his banes glowres back. Strang, present dool
ruggs at my hairt. Lichtlie this gin ye daur:
here Robert Burns knelt and kissed the mool.

from Selected Poems 1966

Elegy

They are lang deid, folk that I used to ken,
their firm-set lips aa mowdert and agley,
sherp-tempert een rusty amang the cley:
they are baith deid, thae wycelike, bienlie men,

heidmaisters, that had been in pouer for ten
or twenty year afore fate's taiglie wey
brocht me, a young, weill-harnit, blate and fey
new-cleckit dominie, intill their den.

roseirs rose-bushes	*leam* gleam	*haar* mist
glaur mud	*haps* covers	*glowres* glares
dool sorrow	*ruggs* tugs	*lichtlie* despise
mool earth of a grave		
mowdert decayed	*agley* awry	*bienlie* prosperous
taiglie tangled	*weill-harnit* well-equipped with brains	
blate bashful	*fey* foreseeing trouble	*new-cleckit* hatched

Ane tellt me it was time I learnt to write –
round-haund, he meant – and saw about my hair:
I mind of him, beld-heidit, wi a kyte.

Ane sneerit quarterly – I cuidna square
my savings bank – and sniftert in his spite.
Weill, gin they arena deid, it's time they were.

from Selected Poems 1966

Fable (Twa' mice)

Twa mice, that never ocht had kennd
bit puirtith cauld, cam in the end,
by rare guid fortune, sae they thocht,
til ane auld hous whaur mice had wrocht
their hidey-holes in sic a maze,
it micht hae gane back til the days
of thon seafaring patriarch
that shairpt his teeth on Noah's Ark.
Forbye, a maist byordnar treat,
they cuid smell somethin nice to eat,
sae baith thegither cried, 'It's clear
the Revolution's happent here.'
They cleikit pinkies as we dae,
and wished a wish to keep it sae.
Jist then, in cam a muckle rat
and said, 'Git the hell ou'a that.'
Straucht, in ae blink, twa cats cam in;
the food, in fact, wes Warfarin;
as fir the hous they'd aa fand boun,
men cam that day and caa'd it doun.

not previously published

kyte paunch   ane one
kennd known   puirtith poverty   wrocht worked
shairpt sharpened   forbye besides
byordnar extraordinary   cleikit hooked   muckle big
straucht straight   Warfarin brand of rat poison
boun ready

Programme notes

Berlioz' biggest-ever Requiem
for soldiers killed in France's recent war
was finished far too late, so huge a score
that France had won another war by then –
or lost? – no matter; history's a bore.
At any rate, they'd been at it again,
incurring once again the usual losses,
such as we mark with little wooden crosses.
Choir, foghorn, orchestra and four brass bands,
tuned up at last in diatonic prayer,
splendid for anyone who understands
that sort of thing; I'm glad I wasn't there.
Critics in all time since, in many lands,
agree, this Requiem's a great affair
of super-output, multi-decibel,
designed to save two armies' dead from Hell.
Why not, indeed? Why shouldn't it be so?
It makes no difference that I'm tone-deaf,
and couldn't recognise a treble clef,
if music's daughters have not been brought low
by some grave atheist with an iron rod
who wants to stand between ourselves and God.

not previously published

During a music festival

Cantie in seaside simmer on the dunes,
I fling awa my dowp of cigarette
whaur bairns hae biggit castles out of sand
and watch the reik rise frae the parapet.

Suddenlike I am back in Libya:
yon's the escarpment, and a bleizan plane,
the wee white speck that feeds the luift wi reik,
dirkins a horror-pictur on my brain.

And aye the reik bleeds frae the warld's rim
as it has duin frae Bablyon and Troy,
London, Bonn, Edinbro, time eftir time.
And great Beethoven sang a Hymn to Joy.

from Selected Poems 1966

Mune-gyte

They're faur left to theirsels – the auld wife leuch –
    a bonnie cairry-on,
we aye hae lunatics eneuch
    wi ae auld-farrant mune.
The lyft will sune be chockablock
    wi tinny-munes galore,
rockets, deid dowgs and siclike trock,
    and bleepan bits of wire,
aa trackit-doun on Jodrell Bank.
    The Baptist's cry sounds odd,
nou that we're nearer til the mune
    and ferder aye frae God.

from Selected Poems 1966

---

reik smoke   *luift* sky   *dirkins* darkens (making a film)
mune-gyte moon-mad   *ae* one   *auld-farrant* old-fashioned
dowgs dogs in space

Sisyphus

Bumpity doun in the corrie gaed whuddran the pitiless whun stane.
Sisyphus, pechan and sweitan, disjaskit, forfeuchan and broun'd-aff
sat on the heather a hanlawhile, houpan the Boss didna spy him,
seean the terms of his contract includit nae mention of tea-breaks,
syne at the muckle big scunnersom boulder he trauchlit aince mair.
Ach! hou kenspeckle it was, that he ken'd ilka spreckle and blotch
   on't.
Heavan awa at its wecht, he manhaunnlit the bruitt up the braeface,
takkan the easiest gait he had fand in a fudder of dour years,
haudan awa frae the craigs had affrichtit him maist in his youth-
   heid,
feelan his years aa the same, he gaed cannily, tenty of slipped discs.
Eftir an hour and a quarter he warslit his wey to the brae's heid,
hystit his boulder richt up on the tap of the cairn – and it stude
   there!
streikit his length on the chuckie-stanes, houpan the Boss wadna spy
   him,
had a wee look at the scenery, feenisht a pie and a cheese-piece.
Whit was he thinkan about, that he jist gied the boulder a wee shove?
Bumpity doun in the corrie gaed whuddran the pitiless whun stane,
Sisyphus dodderan eftir it, shair of his cheque at the month's end.

from Selected Poems 1966

whuddran thudding	*pechan* puffing	*disjaskit* worn out
forfeuchan exhausted	*hanlawhile* short time	*scunnersom* disgusting
trauchlit toiled (with difficulty)	*kenspeckle* familiar	
fudder large number	*tenty* careful	*warslit* wrestled
streikit stretched	*dodderan* moving slowly and unsteadily	

Norman MacCaig

Born in Edinburgh in 1910, Norman MacCaig was educated at the Royal High School and Edinburgh University where he took an Honours degree in Classics. Except for War Service, his career has been spent in teaching. After secondment to Edinburgh University in 1967 as first Fellow in Creative Writing he returned briefly to school teaching before taking up a permanent appointment as Lecturer in Creative Writing at the University of Stirling.

MacCaig was already writing poetry in the 1930s. Along with J. F. Hendry, G. S. Fraser and Henry Treece, he was a member of the Apocalypse group (responsible for two anthologies *The New Apocalypse* 1939 and *The White Horseman* 1941) who were attempting to emancipate poetry (amongst other things) from the dominant influences of Auden, both political and social. That Norman MacCaig succeeded in finding for himself and for the reader a splendid new poetry is evident from the many volumes he has published since 1946. In his early volumes *Far Cry* 1945 and *The Inward Eye* 1946, it is hard to detect any pattern. He was in that early period drawn to surrealism and his verse is full of obscurity but, of course, he was still learning his trade. He has never been a poet to revise (as George MacKay Brown is) but rather tries to improve in the next poem or next volume.

There were nine years between *The Inward Eye* and *Riding Lights* 1955; in the latter volume the essential MacCaig is seen in abundance for the first time.

G. S. Fraser states that Norman MacCaig is a poet involved with the self as subject and object in most of his work. The title of a recent volume of MacCaig, *A Man in My Position*, suggests that everything is viewed from his own particular angle by one of many selves he knows to be inside his skin. Norman MacCaig, the Classicist, is in the tradition of the philosophical Scot, engaged in metaphysical enquiry, exploring the relationship of the observer and the observed and the world and himself. One side of him looks at another through the lens of a landscape or external object, often in a comic way as in 'Other Self'. In the final stanzas of 'Summer Farm' MacCaig writes:

Self under self, a pile of selves I stand
Threaded on time, and with metaphysic hand
Lift the farm like a lid and see
Farm within farm, and in the centre, me.

MacCaig has the speculative power, and the wit of the metaphysicals and is most like Donne in his syllogistic skill in coming to surprise but logical conclusions. Norman MacCaig has said, 'I am a happy man . . . and nearly all the poems I write are in fact praising things.' He enjoys writing about places and in his descriptions of the Scottish Highlands and the Hebrides, especially seascapes and mountain scenes, he manifests the sharp vision of the painter (he is a skilled painter himself) and combines with this a sensuous awareness of the qualities of the scene. His feeling for the Highlands may have come from his mother, who was a Gaelic speaker.

His sensitivity to sounds, smells and tastes is positively Keatsian. He views the subject in an unusual way with the light of a powerful imagination as in 'Byres' where the simple scene is invested with the aura of the Nativity. Hugh MacDairmid has spoken of the insufficient effort on Norman MacCaig's part to deal with the great and pressing problems of our time. This is certainly not true of his later volumes *Rings on a Tree* 1968 and *A Man in My Position* 1969. Since his visits to Italy and USA, there has come into his poetry a new note of social criticism and an increasing awareness of the march of uncivilisation in the USA. He observes in 'Last Night in New York',

The sun goes up on Edinburgh,
Manhattan goes up on the sun.
Her buildings overtop Arthur's Seat.
And are out of date as soon as a
newspaper.

In 'Assisi', his sympathy goes out to the misshapen dwarf while his scorn is turned on the priest who, ignoring the plight of the human figure, 'scattered the grain of the word'. In his poem for TV, 'A Man in Assynt', he looks on the depopulation of the west Highlands which he loves so dearly, in the same searching critical manner as he does on the American and Italian scenes.

Norman MacCaig is the outstanding craftsman among Scottish poets writing in English. He is the master of the felicitous phrase and the surprise ending. He also displays a deftness in handling a variety of metres. His later employment of free verse does not seem to have blunted his edge but has given him scope for a wider range of subject. It is difficult to keep pace with his enormous output of fine poems – no fewer than ten volumes have appeared up to 1970. The publication of his *Selected Poems* 1971 will give the reader a better opportunity to appreciate his uniqueness, versatility and his stature as an important poet of the English-speaking world.

Summer farm

Straws like tame lightnings lie about the grass
And hang zigzag on hedges. Green as glass
The water in the horse-trough shines.
Nine ducks go wobbling by in two straight lines.

A hen stares at nothing with one eye,
Then picks it up. Out of an empty sky
A swallow falls and, flickering through
The barn, dives up again into the dizzy blue.

I lie, not thinking, in the cool, soft grass,
Afraid of where a thought might take me – as
This grasshopper with plated face
Unfolds his legs and finds himself in space.

Self under self, a pile of selves I stand
Threaded on time, and with metaphysic hand
Lift the farm like a lid and see
Farm within farm, and in the centre, me.

from Riding Lights 1955

November night, Edinburgh

The night tinkles like ice in glasses.
Leaves are glued to the pavement with frost.
The brown air fumes at the shop windows,
Tries the doors, and sidles past.

I gulp down winter raw. The heady
Darkness swirls with tenements.
In a brown fuzz of cottonwool
Lamps fade up crags, die into pits.

Frost in my lungs is harsh as leaves
Scraped up on paths. – I look up, there,
A high roof sails, at the mast-head
Fluttering a grey and ragged star.

The world's a bear shrugged in his den.
It's snug and close in the snoring night.
And outside like chrysanthemums
The fog unfolds its bitter scent.

from The Sinai Sort 1957

Nude in a fountain

Clip-clop go water-drops and bridles ring –
Or, visually a gauze of water, blown
About and falling and blown about, discloses
Pudicity herself in shameless stone,
In an unlikely world of shells and roses.

On shaven grass a summer's litter lies
Of paper bags and people. One o'clock
Booms on the leaves with which the trees are quilted
And wades away through air, making it rock
On flowerbeds that have blazed and dazed and wilted.

Light perches, preening, on the handle of a pram
And gasps on paths and runs along a rail
And whitely, brightly in a soft diffusion
Veils and unveils the naked figure, pale
As marble in her stone and stilled confusion.

And nothing moves except one dog that runs,
A red rag in a black rag, round and round
And that long helmet-plume of water waving,
In which the four elements, hoisted from the ground,
Become this grace, the form of their enslaving.

Meeting and marrying in the midmost air
Is mineral assurance of them all;
White doldrum on blue sky; a pose of meaning
Whose pose is what is explicit; a miracle
Made, and made bearable, by the water's screening.

The drops sigh, singing, and, still sighing, sing
Gently a leaning song. She makes no sound.
They veil her, not with shadows, but with brightness;
Till, gleam within a glitter, they expound
What a tall shadow is when it is whiteness.

A perpetual modification of itself
Going on around her is her; her hand is curled
Round more than a stone breast; and she discloses
The more than likely in an unlikely world
Of dogs and people and stone shells and roses.

from A Common Grace 1960

Goat

The goat, with amber dumb-bells in his eyes,
The blasé lecher, inquisitive as sin,
White sarcasm walking, proof against surprise,

The nothing like him goat, goat-in-itself,
Idea of goatishness made flesh, pure essence
In idle masquerade on a rocky shelf –

Hangs upside down from lushest grass to twitch
A shrivelled blade from the cliff's barren chest,
And holds the grass well lost; the narrowest niche

Is frame for the devil's face; the steepest thatch
Of barn or byre is pavement to his foot;
The last, loved rose a prisoner to his snatch;

And the man in his man-ness, passing, feels suddenly
Hypocrite found out, hearing behind him that
Vulgar vibrato, thin derisive me-eh.

from A Common Grace 1960

Feeding ducks

One duck stood on my toes.
The others made watery rushes after bread
Thrown by my momentary hand; instead,
She stood duck-still and got far more than those.

An invisible drone boomed by
With a beetle in it; the neighbour's yearning bull
Bugled across five fields. And an evening full
Of other evenings quietly began to die.

And my everlasting hand
Dropped on my hypocrite duck her grace of bread.
And I thought, 'The first to be fattened, the first to be dead',
Till my gestures enlarged, wide over the darkening land.

from A Common Grace 1960

Edinburgh courtyard in July

Hot light is smeared as thick as paint
On these ramshackle tenements. Stones smell
Of dust. Their hoisting into quaint
Crowsteps, corbels, carved with fool and saint,
Hold fathoms of heat, like water in a well.

Cliff-dwellers have poked out from their
High cave-mouths brilliant rags on drying-lines;
They hang still, dazzling in the glare,
And lead the eye up, ledge by ledge, to where
A chimney's tilted helmet winks and shines.

And water from a broken drain
Splashes a glassy hand out in the air
That breaks in an unbraiding rain
And falls still fraying, to become a stain
That spreads by footsteps, ghosting everywhere.

from A Common Grace 1960

Byre

The thatched roof rings like heaven where mice
Squeak small hosannahs all night long,
Scratching its golden pavements, skirting
The gutter's crystal river-song.

Wild kittens in the world below
Glare with one flaming eye through cracks,
Spurt in the straw, are tawny brooches
Splayed on the chests of drunken sacks.

The dimness becomes darkness as
Vast presences come mincing in,
Swagbellied Aphrodites, swinging
A silver slaver from each chin.

D

And all is milky, secret, female.
Angels are hushed and plain straws shine.
And kittens miaow in circles, stalking
With tail and hindleg one straight line.

from A Round of Applause 1962

The streets of Florence

Tired of these ordinary heads carrying
From somewhere else to somewhere or other
Their ordinary ambitions and lusts and boredoms,
I turned aside into the Uffizi Gallery
And submerged myself in the throng
Of undying presences, created once
In the minds of great painters and
Continuously creating themselves ever since.

When I went out again
Into the steep sunlight, I saw with astonishment
These undying presences had climbed down
From the walls and with an unconvincing
Change of clothes were carrying
Their extraordinary heads from one
Great rendezvous to another.

I, then? What am I
A continuing creation of? What Hebridean
Island and what century have I failed
To escape from in the dangerous journey
From my first great rendezvous to the one
I have still to keep?

from Surroundings 1966

Assisi

The dwarf with his hands on backwards
Sat, slumped like a half-filled sack
On tiny twisted legs from which
Sawdust might run,
Outside the three tiers of churches built
In honour of St Francis, brother
Of the poor, talker with birds, over whom
He had the advantage
Of not being dead yet.

A priest explained
How clever it was of Giotto
To make his frescoes tell stories
That would reveal to the illiterate the goodness
Of God and the suffering
Of His Son. I understood
The explanation and
The cleverness.

A rush of tourists, clucking contentedly,
Fluttered after him as he scattered
The grain of the word. It was they who had passed
The ruined temple outside, whose eyes
Wept pus, whose back was higher
Than his head, whose lopsided mouth
Said, *Grazie* in a voice as sweet
As a child's when she speaks to her mother
Or a bird's when it spoke
To St Francis.

from Surroundings 1966

Smuggler

Watch him when he opens
His bulging words – justice,
Fraternity, freedom, internationalism, peace,
Peace, peace. Make it your custom
To pay no heed
To his frank look, his visas, his stamps
And signatures. Make it
Your duty to spread out their contents
In a clear light.

Nobody with such luggage
Has nothing to declare.

from Surroundings 1966

A man in Assynt
A poem for television

Glaciers, grinding West, gouged out
these valleys, rasping the brown sandstone,
and left, on the hard rock below – the
ruffled foreland –
this frieze of mountains filed
on the blue air – Stac Polly,
Cul Beag, Cul Mor, Suilven,
Canisp – a frieze and
a litany.

Who owns this landscape?
Has owning anything to do with love?
For it and I have a love-affair, so nearly human
we even have quarrels. –
When I intrude too confidently
it rebuffs me with a wind like a hand
or puts in my way
a quaking bog or a loch
where no loch should be. Or I turn stonily

away, refusing to notice
the rouged rocks, the mascara
under a dripping ledge, even
the tossed, the stony limbs waiting.

I can't pretend
it gets sick for me in my absence,
though I get
sick for it. Yet I love it
with special gratitude, since
it sends no letters, is never
jealous and, expecting nothing
from me, gets nothing but
cigarette packets and footprints.

Who owns this landscape? –
The millionaire who bought it or
the poacher staggering downhill in the early morning
with a deer on his back?

Who possesses this landscape? –
The man who bought it or
I who am possessed by it?

False question, for
this landscape is
masterless
and intractable in any terms
that are human.
It is docile only to the weather
and its indefatigable lieutenants –
wind, water and frost.
The wind whets the high ridges
and stunts silver birches and alders.
Rain falling down meets
springs gushing up –
they gather and carry down to the Minch
tons of sour soil, making bald
the bony scalp of Cul Mor. And frost
thrusts his hand in cracks and, clenching his fist,
bursts open the sandstone plates,
the armour of Suilven:
he bleeds stones down chutes and screes,
smelling of gunpowder.

Or has it come to this,
that this dying landscape belongs
to the dead, the crofters and fighters
and fishermen whose larochs
sink into the bracken
by Loch Assynt and Loch Crocach? –
to men trampled under the hoofs of sheep
and driven by deer to
the ends of the earth – to men whose loyalty
was so great it accepted their own betrayal
by their own chiefs and whose descendants now
are kept in their place
by English businessmen and the indifference
of a remote and ignorant government . . .

from A Man in My Position 1969

Crossing the border

I sit with my back to the engine, watching
the landscape pouring away out of my eyes.
I think I know where I'm going and have
some choice in the matter.

I think, too, that this was a country
of bog-trotters, of moss-troopers,
fired ricks and rooftrees in the black night – glinting
on tossed horns and red blades.
I think of lives
bubbling into the harsh grass.

What difference now?
I sit with my back to the future, watching
time pouring away into the past. I sit, being helplessly
lugged backwards
through the debatable lands of history, listening
to the execrations, the scattered cries, the
falling of rooftrees
in the lamentable dark.

from Rings on a Tree 1968

Hotel room, 12th floor

This morning I watched from here
a helicopter skirting like a damaged insect
the Empire State Building, that
jumbo size dentist's drill, and landing
on the roof of the PanAm skyscraper.
But now midnight has come in
from foreign places. Its uncivilised darkness
is shot at by a million lit windows, all
ups and acrosses.

But midnight is not
so easily defeated. I lie in bed, between
a radio and a television set, and hear
the wildest of warwhoops continually ululating through
the glittering canyons and gulches –
police cars and ambulances racing
to the broken bones, the harsh screaming
from coldwater flats, the blood
glazed on sidewalks.

The frontier is never
somewhere else. And no stockades
can keep the midnight out.

from Rings on a Tree 1968

Sydney Goodsir Smith

Sydney Goodsir Smith, one of the leaders of the Scottish Renaissance and the Lallans Movement, had an unlikely upbringing for a Scots poet. Born in 1915 in New Zealand (of a Scottish mother), he was later educated at Malvern College and the University of Oxford. On his father's appointment to the Chair of Forensic Medicine at Edinburgh, Sydney Goodsir Smith continued his studies at Edinburgh University after which he settled in the capital where he became, in the words of Hugh MacDiarmid, 'the Burns de nos jours'.

A born lyricist, Goodsir Smith, through the influence of Hugh MacDiarmid, took to Lallans. In the 'Epistle to John Guthrie', he explains why he chose to write Scots rather than English and indeed makes out a splendid case for Lallans. His attitude to language is only one indication of his rebellion against the conventions of an established society. He feels there is no place for the poet in contemporary society. Regarding himself as outcast, he refuses to accept the conventions and morality of the society which has rejected him.

In his earlier volumes *Skail Wind* 1941 and *The Wanderer and other Poems* 1943 he is still searching for an adequate medium to express his powerful feelings and aspirations. In the volume *Deevil's Waltz* 1946, he is already in full possession of his poetic equipment and from then follows a succession of volumes including the magnificent *Under the Eildon Tree* 1948. The tender, tragic and the uproarious mingle in this remarkable set of twenty-four elegies on the universal theme of love. In 1965 appeared *Kynd Kittock's Land*, a racy TV poem about Edinburgh. In 1969 was published *Fifteen Poems and a Play*.

Possessing a strong dramatic talent, Goodsir Smith has written a number of fine plays, notably *The Wallace*, broadcast in 1959 and produced in the Assembly Hall in the 1960 Edinburgh Festival,

104

and *The Stick-up*, a play of Glasgow slum life in the 1930s which recently became the subject of a successful opera by Robin Orr, entitled *Full Circle*.

Goodsir Smith is steeped in Scottish tradition and literature and has consciously striven to contribute to and develop the Scottish poetic heritage. He is deeply read in Scottish poetry from the Middle Ages to MacDiarmid, having a particular interest in Gavin Douglas, Dunbar, Henryson, and Fergusson and Burns. This, rather than English, is the literature from which he draws inspiration. He also exploits Celtic and Classical mythology for subject material. He is, at the same time, fully aware of the contemporary world including its literature, reading widely in French, Italian and Russian. As well as drawing on Scottish literature, he continues to develop Scots, employing not only the language of today with its many racy expressions but the whole range of vocabulary available from the Makars and their successors up to the time of Burns. No modern writer has handled the Scots language more effectively over a wide range of subjects.

Goodsir Smith the scholar and critic has written a valuable *Introduction to Scottish Literature* and has edited a critical work on Robert Fergusson. He has also edited *Selected Poems of Gavin Douglas* (Saltire Poets), *Burns's Poems and Songs* (Faber) and *The Merry Muses of Caledonia*. A connoisseur of the arts and friend of painters, Sydney Goodsir Smith was for some years Art Critic of *The Scotsman*.

Epistle to John Guthrie
(*who had blamed the poet for writing in Scots
'which no one speaks'*)

We've come intil a gey queer time
Whan scrievin Scots is near a crime,
'There's no one speaks like that', they fleer,
– But wha the deil spoke like King Lear?

scrievin writing   *fleer* sneer

And onyweys doon Canongate
I'll tak ye slorpin pints till late,
Ye'll hear Scots there as raff and slee –
It's no the point, sae that'll dae.

Ye'll fin the leid, praps no the fowth,
The words're there, praps no the ferlie;
For he wha'ld rant wi Rabbie's mouth
Maun leave his play-pen unco erlie.

Nane cud talk lik Gawen Douglas writes,
He hanna the vocablerie,
Nor cud he flyte as Dunbar flytes –
Yir argy-bargy's tapsalteerie!

Did Johnnie Keats whan he was drouth
Ask 'A beaker full o the warm South'?
Fegs no, he leaned across the bar
An called for 'A point o bitter, Ma!'

But the Suddron's noo a sick man's leid,
Alang the flattest plains it stots;
Tae reach the hills his fantice needs
This bard maun tak the wings o Scots.

And so, dear John, ye jist maun dree
My Scots; for English, man, 's near deid,
See the weeshy-washy London bree
An tell me then whaes bluid is reid!

But mind, nae poet eer writes 'common speech',
Ye'll fin eneuch o yon in prose;
His realm is heich abune its reach –
Jeez! wha'ld use ale for Athol Brose?

from Skail Wind 1941

slorpin swilling   *raff* abundant   *slee* witty   *leid* tongue
fowth whole   *ferlie* magic   *flytes* scolds
tapsalteerie upside down   *fegs* faith   *Suddron* English
fantice imagination   *dree* put up with   *bree* brew

The mither's lament

What care I for the leagues o sand,
The prisoners and the gear theyve won?
My darlin liggs amang the dunes
Wi mony a mither's son.

Doutless he deed for Scotland's life;
Doutless the statesmen dinna lee;
But och tis sair begrutten pride
And wersh the wine o victorie!

from The Deevil's Waltz 1946

Lament for R. W.

There's nae philosophie I hae
Can blaw the wund anither wey,
There's nae gran thochts my brain can spin
Wull skail the mirk frae out my minn,
There's neer a word can heal a scaur
   Or stap the war.

There's neer a prayer wull fly him hame
Nor yet a certain yin tae blame;
When the guilty ramp the innocent pay
– Dick's shot doun owre Norroway;
There's neer a spell can lown the brak
   Or fetch him back.

But let a curse aye rest on aa
Whaes avarice gruppit him awa;
Vengeance graiths for the michty few;
The skime o bluid-guilt weets their brou –
But och nae tears nor cuse can speed
   Dick hame frae the deid.

from The Deevil's Waltz 1946

begrutten tear-stained	*wersh* bitter
skail scatter, disperse	*lown* abate, calm
graiths makes ready, prepares	*skime* reflected light

Sahara

I

Inexorable on ye stride,
Fate, like a desert wund;
Agin your vast unpassioned pride
I pit ma saul and haund,
As the wild Bedouin
Tykes gowl at the mune.

II

March, ye luveless Cailleach, blaw
Till the dumbest, mirkest end,
And whan the yerth's a blastit skau
As toom Sahara brunt and blind
There, daft and damned wi raivan ee,
Adam, greinan tae be free.

The Deevil's Waltz 1946

Largo

Ae boat anerlie nou
Fishes frae this shore,
Ae black drifter lane
Riggs the cramasie daw –
Aince was a fleet, and nou
Ae boat alane gaes out.

War or peace, the trawlers win
And the youth turns awa
Bricht wi baubles nou
And thirled to factory or store;
Their faithers fished their ain,
Unmaistered; – ane remains.

tykes dogs   *gowl* howl   *Cailleach* lit. old woman;
the old Grey woman demon of storm and winter
mirkest darkest   *yerth* earth   *skau* ruin, chaos
toom empty   *brunt* burnt   *greinan* yearning
anerlie only   *riggs* furrows   *cramasie* crimson
daw dawn   *thirled* enslaved

And never the clock rins back,
The free days are owre;
The warld shrinks, we luik
Mair t'oor maisters ilka hour –
Whan yon lane boat I see
Daith and rebellion blinn ma ee!

from The Deevil's Waltz 1946

Elegy VIII

I had a luve walked by the sea,
The waterfront at eenin,
Sol was a gowden pennie at our side
A bare league awa.
A wee boat wi a broun sail
Left the pier juist at our feet
And sailed awa intil the sunset
Silentlie, the water like a keekin-gless.
We spak nae word ava.
My luve turned til me wi her een
Owre-rin wi greit, and mine
Were weet wi the like mysterie.
We stude by the Pharos there
A lang while or the sun dwyned doun
And the gray-green simmer dayligaun
Closed about the hyne.
Syne it grew cauld, and in my airms
I felt her trummlan
Wi the like undeemous mysterie did steek
My craig, sae's I coudna speak.

from Under the Eildon Tree 1948

ilka each	*blinn* blind	*keekin-gless* mirror
ava at all	*owre-rin wi greit* running over with tears	
or before	*dwyned* declined	*dayligaun* dusk
hyne harbour	*syne* afterwards	*trummlan* trembling
undeemous unknown and incomprehensible		
steek close	*craig* throat	

Hamewith
'En ma fin est mon commencement.' –
Marie Stuart

Man at the end
Til the womb wends,
Fisher til sea,
Hunter to hill,
Miner the pit seeks,
Sodjer the bield.

As bairn on breist
Seeks his first need
Makar his thocht prees,
Doer his deed,
Sanct his peace
And sinner remeid.

Man in dust is lain
And exile wins hame.

from So Late into the Night 1952

King and Queen o the fowr airts

O, King and Queen o the fowr airts,
My love and I yon day,
They sang o us in Tara Haas,
They carolled in Cathay.

For us the mirkie lift was gowd,
The causie gowd beneath,
Emerants drapt frae ilka tree
And siller ran the water o Leith.

hamewith homeward   *til* to   *sodjer* soldier
bield shelter, refuge   *makar* poet   *prees* attains
sanct saint   *remeid* relief, redress
airts directions, four quarters   *mirkie lift* dark sky
emerants emeralds   *siller* silver

The Dean Brig lowpt a Hieland Fling
Our regal whim to gratifie,
Schir Wattie sclimmed his steeple's tap
The better to view sic majestie.

Och, we were the sun and sickle mune,
The wee speugs triumphed round our wey,
Sanct Giles cast doun his muckle croun
And aa the damned made holiday.

Tamburlane was a shilpiskate,
Ozymandias a parvenu,
Our Empire o the Embro streets
Owrepassed the dwaums o Xanadu.

But fient the pleasure-dome we fand,
Waif peacocks mang the laicher breeds,
We ained the birlin mapamound
— But damn the neuk to lay our heids.

The birds hae nests, the tods dens,
The baillie skouks aneath his stane,
But we, the minions o the race,
We hadna howff and we hadna hame.

Ay, King and Queen o the fowr airts,
Our crounit heids abune the cloud,
Our bed yon nicht was the munelicht gress
— I wadna changed for Holyrood!

from So Late into the Night 1952

lowpt danced
Schir Wattie Sir Walter Scott (Monument in Princes Street)
speugs sparrows
Sanct Giles . . . croun the crown tower on the cathedral
shilpiskate nonentity   *dwaums* dreams
feint the devil a . . .   *laicher* lower
mapamound globe   *neuk* corner   *tods* foxes
skouks skulks   *howff* shelter   *abune* above

Cokkils

Doun throu the sea
   Continuallie
A rain o cokkils, shells
   Rains doun
Frae the ceaseless on-ding
O' the reefs abune –
   Continuallie.

Slawlie throu millenia
Biggan on the ocean bed
Their ain subaqueous Himalaya
Wi a fine white rain o shells
Faa'an continuallie
   Wi nae devall.

Sae, in my heid as birdsang
Faas throu simmer treen
Is the thocht o my luve
Like the continual rain
O' cokkils throu the middle seas
   Wi nae devall –
The thocht o my true-luve
   Continuallie.

from Cokkils 1953

on-ding battering   *devall* respite   *treen* trees

The grace of God and the meth drinker

There ye gang, ye daft
And doitit dotterel, ye saft
Crazed outland skalrag saul
In your bits and ends o winnockie duds
Your fyled and fozie-fousome clouts
And fou's a fish, crackt and craftie-drunk
Wi bleerit reid-rimmed
Ee and slaveran crozie mou
Dwaiblan owre the causie like a ship
Storm-toss'd i' the Bay of Biscay O
At-sea indeed and hauf-seas-owre
Up-til-the-thrapple's-pap
Or up-til-the-crosstrees-sunk –
    Wha kens? Wha racks?
Hidderie-hetterie stouteran in a dozie dwaum
O' ramsh reid-biddie – Christ!
        The stink
O' jake ahint him, a mephitic
Rouk o miserie, like some unco exotic
Perfume o the Orient no juist sae easilie tholit
By the bleak barbarians o the Wast
But subtil, acrid, jaggan the nebstrous
Wi'n owrehailan ugsome guff, maist delicat,
Like in scent til the streel o a randie gib . . .
      O-hone-a-ree!

doited crazed   *dotterel* dotard   *outland* outlandish, uncouth
skalrag vagabond   *winnockie* windowy (full of holes)
duds rags   *fozie-fousome* dirty and disgusting
clouts clothes   *crozie* whining, wheedling
dwaiblan shambling   *causie* street
thrapple's pap Adam's apple   *hidderie-hetterie* hither and thither
stouteran staggering   *dwaum* brown study, day-dream
ramsh fiery   *reid-biddie* methylated spirits mixed with cheap wine
jake 'reid-biddie'   *ahint* behind   *rouk* thick heavy mist
unco uncommonly   *tholit* endured   *nebstrou* nostril
owrehailan overwhelming   *ugsome* repulsive   *guff* stink
streel urine   *gib* tom-cat

His toothless gums, his lips, bricht cramasie
A schere-bricht slash o bluid
A schene like the leaman gleid o rubies
Throu the gray-white stibble
O' his blank unrazit chafts, a hangman's
Heid, droolie wi gob, the bricht een
Sichtless, cannie, blythe, and slee –
                              Unkennan.

Ay,
        Puir gangrel!
                              There
– But for the undeemous glorie and grace
O' a mercifu omnipotent majestic God
Superne eterne and sceptred in the firmament
Whartil the praises o the leal rise
Like incense aye about Your throne,
Ayebydan, thochtless, and eternallie hauf-drunk
Wi nectar, Athole-brose, ambrosia – nae jake for
        You –
              God there! –
But for the 'bunesaid unsocht grace, unprayed-
        for,
Undeserved –
                        Gangs,
                              Unregenerate,
                                    Me.

from Figs and Thistles 1959

cramasie crimson
schere-bricht vividly bright   *leaman* flaming   *gleid* fire
unrazit unshaven   *chafts* jaws   *droolie* slobbering
slee cunning   *unkennan* unknowing, unaware
gangrel vagabond   *undeemous* unknown and incomprehensible
superne above all   *leal* loyal, faithfull   *gangs* goes
ayebydan everlasting   *bunesaid* above said

My world in nether winter

My world in nether winter is the sun
Barred in a cell and dernit dull in yerth,
The cache is tint, the road unmapt
And dumb wi babban-quaas its dule and rime;
Sol is dowsit dim, deid not, but hapt
And hainit close or Cocorico bells rebirth
In the clean white clout o the Lamb.

Maybe in the morn o beasts and flouers
The outspate o the gleid releas't
Will flush aa winter's dubs wi sun —
In the Lyon's vessels deep it bydes the hour
And bluid, nou silent, sings in the catacomb
Whar leaf na life can neither sleep
— E'en in this sunless world o nether winter's deep.

from Figs and Thistles 1959

Credo

Celebrate the seasons
Haud after veritie
Find your equilibrium
And tell what happened ye.

Syne lay doun in a hole
Be the worms' victual
The tyke has had his day
And this is all.

What mair is there ye wiss?
Luve's memorie dwynes, the prufe
Is there for ye that watch
The hevins muve.

dernit concealed	*yerth* earth	*tint* lost	
babban-quaas quagmires	*dule* sorrow		
dowsit extinguished	*hainit* preserved	*or* before	
gleid fire	*dubs* puddles		
syne then	*tyke* dog	*wiss* know	*dwynes* wastes away

Tak aa the praise
Put bye the blame
Bard sing on
In the goddess' name.

Ne'er seek her out
Hers be the advance
But name thy bruckle barque
Bonne Esperance.

Gey aft she'll gie ye
Stanes for breid
But whiles her gift
Is life frae deid.

Celebrate the seasons
And the Muse that rules
Aa truth is dream but this
As dreamers fules.

Luve is the infant treason
O' the saikless saul
Luve is the black dirk
Sheath't in the hairt of all.

Hairt can nocht live athout
This traitor's skaith
Ye can dee a thousand nichts
And ne'er ken daith.

Luve was the first was struck
By the goddess mune
The luve she gied she took —
The tides aye rin.

Celebrate the seasons
And the hours that pass
She that rocks the tides
Rocks ye at last.

from Figs and Thistles 1959

bruckle fragile	*esperance* hope		
saikless innocent	*dirk* dagger	*skaith* harm, wound	
gey very	*whiles* at times	*athout* without	*skaith* injury

The kenless strand

My sails by tempest riven
The sea a race
Whar should be lown and lither
Aa's dispeace:

Dispeace o' hairt that visions
Reefs it downa ride,
Dispeace o' mind in rapids
Nane can guide:

And aye a face afore me
And anither face;
Ane, luve's ancient tragedy —
And ane its peace.

Here, on luve's fludetide I run
There, the unkent strand
Abune the seamaws' tireless grief
Ayont, nae hyne, nae end.

from Fifteen Poems and a Play 1969

riven torn	*lown* calm	*lither* smoothness
downa cannot	*unkent* unknown	*abune* above
seamaws seagulls	*ayont* beyond	*hyne* haven

Tom Scott

Tom Scott was born in Glasgow in 1918, the son of a boiler-maker and apprenticed in the building trade. Though his formal education was thus restricted, he showed early literary talent. Francis Scarfe writing in 1941 in *Auden and After* (Routledge) on the Apocalypse, a new poetic movement, said of Tom Scott, then 22, 'He used to be a stonemason and his poetry has a naïve quality unspoilt by the literary background which intrudes into too much poetry today. His writing seems to come from his inner consciousness . . . the simplicity of the poems is deceptive for a great deal of suffering and conflict is to be felt beneath it:

> "I found him drowned on the rock that night
> And the wind high; moonlight it was
> And the hungry sucking of the sea
> At my feet and his clammy head in my breasts
> That were bare as the rock and the sea and the sand."

Tom Scott served in the Second World War seeing service in London during the blitz and later in Nigeria. After demobilisation he engaged in many occupations including that of postman and dish-washer, doing freelance writing in London until 1952, when, on the invitation of Edwin Muir, he spent a year at Newbattle Abbey College, following this with a degree course at Edinburgh University where he gained an Honours M.A. and a Ph.D. He has specialised in mediaeval Scottish poetry but is also very well versed in modern Scottish poetry.

Meantime he has continued to write poetry and has certainly fulfilled his early promise, at the same time retaining in his work the naïve elemental freshness with the great extension of his range after his discovery of Scots. Tom Scott published two earlier volumes of poems, *Seeven poems o' Maister Francis Villon* 1955 and *An Ode til a New Jerusalem* 1956 but it was with the publication of *The*

118

Ship and Ither Poems 1963 that the full range of his subject matter became evident and his command of Scots unquestioned. A university class exercise resulted in a masterly Scots translation of the Anglo-Saxon *Dream of the Rood*. His classical reading produced 'Orpheus', 'Telemakhos' and 'Ithaka'. From his mediaeval studies came the little gem, 'Villanelle de Noël'.

Scott, though fully aware of his poetic ancestry and willing to be influenced by it, has a strong originality which prevents him from writing mere pastiche. In 'Brand the Builder', the subject of which derives from Fergusson and Burns, we have an original picture of Scottish life as it has been, and continues to be lived. Strong but sensitive character drawing and economy of dialogue characterise the work.

Scott has essayed several times the longer poem, notably 'The Ship', an allegorical poem in which he explores man's world, as Hugh MacDiarmid looked on the misty universe with the vision of the drunk man. Tom Scott saw in the *Titanic* the climax and the end of European advancement. So his 'Ship' which grows with the civilisation of Europe founders with the catastrophic 1914-18 War. 'The Ship' is a noble if a not entirely successful essay in a long neglected mode. More recently Tom Scott has published a long anti-war poem 'At the Shrine o' the Unkent Sodger' 1968. Perhaps the polemics are too much for the poetry. Scott maintains that a prose poetry is the best means of conveying his passionate plea for peace and understanding among men.

But when Tom Scott's wrath is smouldering as in 'Jay', a poem written in response to what the poet regarded as a scurrilous attack on him, he is on his mettle. The reply is careful and calculated and the description of the Jay accurate in all details, with digs asklent at the man behind the bird and thus he cuts his opponent down to size.

As editor, commentator and scholar, Tom Scott's output has been considerable. Editor of *The Penguin Book of Scottish Verse*, joint editor of the *Oxford Book of Scottish Verse* and author of a critical study of the poems of William Dunbar — these are a few of his achievements.

Adam

I cannae mind the wrang they say I did,
The screiver lee'd; but ken that but for it
Our kind had ne'er been born. Could it no be
That birth itsel wes aa the crime, the bairn's
Rebellion at the womb? And syne expulsion
Intil the tuim anxietie o space,
Dependent on the undependable,
The soil accursed, and me cursed intil toil,
A sword forbiddan ilka wey led back.

Lanely we wandert, cursed for an unkent sin,
The wound in my side caaed Eve at my shouder tall,
The Faa til life her life-lot aye to bear,
My love o her to begin and end in pain,
And aa a joyous sorrow in between.

Wes this rejection meant, or duis the saul
Miscaa every gain frae sense o loss?
I canna think that life itsel's a sin
Wi death nocht but the wey that we atone.
I think that God intendit nae sic thing,
But we oursels misdreamed our progress sin
Because we moved frae pleisure intil pain.

And nae wey back, aa roads a leadin on.
Lang, lang, I cuist mysel agin
Thon adamantine yett, thon fleeran sword,
And fell back aye in bluid melled aye wi tears,
The terrible rejection sair to bear,
My ain sword uisless by yon awesome blade,
Yet by dependence forced to try to win
Re-entrance til my paradise again.

screiver writer	*tuim* empty	*ilka* each
unkent unknown	*frae* from	
cuist cast	*yett* gate	*fleeran* flaming
melled mingled	*awesome* terrifying	

Sae my story's been. Hevin on my mind,
Rejectit for my pouerlessness, I planned
To seize the pouer o God, to Satan doun
The Author frae his lordship owre the warld,
Omnipotence the key til Eden's yett,
And dragged in pain my past-tormentit mind
Throu centuries o earthly darg and sweat,
Gleg to see in some sun-lightened plain
The place that I had come frae sae lang syne,
Yet scarcelins noticean the comely earth's
Likeness til itsel – its guidness in itsel.

Until it broke intil my sicht, the licht
O day dispellan Eden's muinlicht glaumour,
And I surrendrit aa thon vain pretence,
Wes nae mair God, nae mair afraid to be
Alane, shut out, nor envied God possession
o whit he'd made his ane – nae langer strove
Wi angels to return, nor feared their sword,
And fand whit peace I could in bein man.

from The Ship and Ither Poems 1963

Villanelle de Noël

The Robin owre aa birds is blest
At this time of the year, Nowel:
The bluid o Christ is on his breist.

Frae Sicily til Hammerfest
The bairns relate the sely tale,
That the Robin owre aa birds is blest,

For on Calvarie he tried to wrest
Frae Yeshu's palm the cruel nail:
The bluid o Christ is on his breist.

darg toil   *gleg* happy   *syne* before
scarcelins hardly   *sely* blessed

Sensyne he's been Yuill's dearest guest,
Nae ither sae welcome as himsel:
The Robin owre aa birds is blest.

He wears the Yuilltide like a vest,
And his sang's the peal o a ferlie bell:
The bluid o Christ is on his breist.

Nae starred and medalled hero's chest
Can eer wi greater merit swell:
The Robin owre aa birds is blest.
The bluid o Christ is on his breist.

from The Scotsman

Jay
(*Garrulus Glandarius*)

No for him the lyric gift o sang
Alane identifees the outwaled bard:
Yon bird's a realist, and his voice
A harsk and realistic skriek
Like linoleum tearan,
Tho whiles he chuckles and clucks
As owre some private joke,
Or wheeples and pyow-myows in his neb.

But tho nae Orpheus in voice he hes an ee
A bead o slaty-blue
That glints warily out
And misses little:
A clever ee that jays the world
Intil a world o his ain conceit.

sensyne since then   *ferlie* wondrous
outwaled outstanding   *neb* beak

He's kittle, mak na dout,
A sleekit, aggressive sidewinder o a bird,
Fit for tricks and treacheries,
Preferran the shade o a wuid til open fields,
As weel he micht, because,
Tho rife eneuch in England,
Here the breed is herried for its habits
By keepers o game, and by game fishers
For its fly feathers.

Whiles his pagan tones are heard
Deep in the mirk o a wuid
Whaur ither birds are scant,
Caain owre his individual notes, emulatin
Nae ither sound but his ain original skraak;
Nae traditionist he, to sit at the feet o the masters,
Yet, tho he claitters awa in wearie repetition,
Self-imitation,
On aucht that really maitters til the race
The fient a word he hes to say but 'skraak'.

Owre lourd on the wing for lang flights,
He's agile eneuch in the trees,
Climbs and clings weel on brainches,
Is cliquish, fond o bickeran pairties.
Nae dangerous liver, he nests aye near the grund,
Well-eneuch established, weel-eneuch theekit –
He hauds his ain in life, and even Gets On.

Aa birds are worth some study,
And sae is he for whom,
His meisurements carefully booked,
I've tailor-made this suitably tuneless ode:
For under the gaudy disguise,
The gew-gaw glitter and the modish feathers,
Yon taxidermist's pet
Is just anither craw.

from Catalyst Vol II, No. 2 1969

---

kittle easily offended   *sleekit* sly, smooth-tongued   *rife* prevalent
mirk dark   *aucht* anything   *the feint* not a single   *lourd* heavy
bickeran quarrelling   *theekit* thatched   *hauds* holds

Orpheus

Ye think yon wes the end?
Yon meetin in the wuids
When Thracian Orpheus heard the drum, the cries,
The whud o the bacchantes' thrangan feet,
And, seik in saul,
Mad to be jyned for aye til his Eurydikee,
Chordit his harp
And gaed to meet them wi a sang –
Ye think yon wes the end?

Na. Eftar the thrang breeled on, red
Fingert, bluidie-mawed, the riven limbs
Quiveran aye amang the martyred gress,
There wes a lull
And throu it syne a roun
And syne as muckle's a moan
And syne a voice,
Yon voice, yon voice o his
That quaetit the forest and its fowk,
That reconcilit lion and lamb,
That ordert the rain,
Spoke frae the grund
And threept in the greitan tree
'Eurydikee! Eurydikee!'

And at the name,
A ferlie thing wes duin.
Thir broken bits o bodie, bits o bane,
Brisket, gash, airm, and droukit hair
Cam thegither as if some will
Mair nor the merely real
Had wrocht on them:
And on yon slauchtert grund wes formed
Orpheus anew,
Orpheus the singer, Orpheus the makar,
Orpheus cleansed o the auld despair.

breeled moved rapidly   *syne* then
threept kept on calling   *ferlie* wonderful   *nor* than
wrocht worked   *halie* holy   *leaman* gleaming

And, by the halie tree,
In the leaman licht o the wuid,
Squired by a houlet, hawk and doo,
Wes his Eurydikee.

They say he made a new sang,
A nobler nor the auld,
And sings it aye in the great haa o the warld.

They say It will never end.

from The Ship and Ither Poems 1963

Auld Sanct Aundrians – Brand the Builder

On winter days, about the gloamin hour,
Whan the knock on the college touer
Is chappan lowsin-time,
And ilka mason packs his mell and tools awa
Ablow his banker, and bien forenenst the waa
The labourer haps the lave o the lime
Wi soppan secks, to keep it frae a frost, or faa
o suddent snaw
Duran the nicht,
And scrawnie craws flap in the shell-green licht
Towards yon bane-bare rickle o trees
That heeze
Up on the knowe abuin the toun,
And the red goun
Is happan mony a student frae the snell nor-easter,
Malcolm Brand, the maister,
Seean the last hand throu the yett
Afore he bars and padlocks it,
Taks ae look round his stourie yaird
Whaur chunks o stane are liggan
Like the ruins o some auld-farrant biggin:

knock clock	*lowsin* (time) stopping	*soppan* soaking
secks sacks	*rickle* loose group	*heeze* heave, rise
happan wrapping	*yett* gate	*auld farrant* old fashioned
biggin building		

Picks a skelf out o his baerd,
Scliffs his tacketty buits, and syne
Clunters hamelins doun the wyn'.

Alang the shore,
The greinan white sea-owsen ramp and roar.

The main street echoes back his clinkan fuit-faas
Frae its waas,
Whaur owre the kerb and causeys yellow licht
Presses back the mirk nicht
As shop-fronts flüde the pavin-stanes in places,
Like the peintit faces
Whures pit on, or actresses, – ay, or meenisters –
To plaese their several customers.
But aye the nordren nicht, cauld as rumour,
Taks command,
Chills the toun wi his militarie humour,
And plots his map o starns wi deadly hand.

Doun by the sea,
Murns the white swaw owre the wrack ayebydanlie.

Stoupan throu the anvil pend
Gaes Brand,
And owre the coort wi the twa-three partan creels,
The birss air fu
o the smell o the sea, and fish, and meltit glue,
Draws up at his door, and syne,
Hawkan his craig afore he gangs in ben.
Gies a bit scrape at the grater wi his heels.
The kail-pat on the hob is hotteran fu
o the usual hash o Irish stew,
And by the grate, a red-haired bewtie frettit thin,
His wife is kaain a spurtle round.
He swaps his buits for his slippers but a sound.
The twa-three bairnies ken to mak nae din
Whan faither's in,
And sit on creepies round about.
Brand gies a muckle yawn, and howks his paper out.

skelf splinter	*clunters* clatters	
hamelins homewards	*sea-owsen* sea-oxen	*mirk* darkness
swaw wave	*ayebydanlie* forever	*pend* lane
partan crab	*birss* sharp	*hawkan his craig* clearing his throat
hotteran fu bubbling	*kaain* turning	*spurtle* porridge stick

Tither side the fire,
The kettle sings like a telephone wire.

'Lord, for what we are about to receive
Help us to be truly thankful – Aimen –
Wumman, ye've pit ingans in't again.'

'Gae wa ye coorse auld hypocrite!
Thank the Lord for your maet, syne grue at it!'

Wi chowks drawn ticht in a speakless scunner
He glowers on her:
Syne on the quate and straucht-faced bairns:
Faulds his paper doun by his eatin-airns,
And, til the loud tick-tockan o the knock,
Sups, and reads, wi nae ither word nor look.

The warld outside
Like a lug-held sea-shell, roars wi the rinnan tide.

The supper owre, Brand redds up for the nicht.
Aiblins there's a schedule for to price,
Or somethin nice
On at the picters – sacont hoose –
Or some poleetical meetin wants his licht,
Or aiblins, wi him t-total aa his life,
No able to seek the pub to flee the wife,
Daunders out the West Sands 'on the loose'.
Whatever tis,
The waater slorps frae his elbucks as he synds his phiz.

And this is aa the life he kens there is?

from Scottish Poetry 1 1966

---

but without   *creepie* slipper   *ingans* onions
syne grue then grumble   *scunner* disgust   *glowers* glares
eatin-airns cutlery   *redds* tidies   *aiblins* perhaps
daunders strolls   *slorps* drops   *synds his phiz* washes his face

The bride

I dreamed a luesome dream o ye yestreen . . .
Ye stuid in dawan fields agin a purpour lift,
And a tree o floueran starns raise frae your croun.
Lown as a simmer sea ye stuid, your breists
Keekan throu the lint-locks o your hair,
And ye were leaman wi a radiance eterne,
My ever-virgin, ever-breedan bride.

Your waddin kiss, the warld your body is,
Are brenned ayebidan in my benmaist hert
As Psyche's oil in Eros' shouther brenned.

Wap your love-spells round me evermair,
Bind me til ye wi your daethless love,
My queen, my queyn, dochter o our God.
Lead me on throu ever grouwan licht, and be
My love, my ain, the guide o the god in me.

In burns o immortal rain baptise me love.

from The Ship and Ither Poems 1963

luesome lovely	*dawan* dawning	*purpour* purple
starns stars	*lift* sky	*lown* calm	*keekan* peeping
leaman gleaming	*eterne* eternal	*waddin* wedding
ayebidan for ever	*benmaist* innermost	*wap* cast
queyn girl	*burns* brooks, streams	

128

Edwin Morgan

Born in Glasgow in 1920, a graduate of Glasgow University (1947), he saw service from 1940 to 46 in the RAMC. At present he is a Senior Lecturer in English at Glasgow University, and he has lectured in German and Hungarian universities. As well as being a poet Morgan is scholar, critic, linguist, translator and broadcaster. His interest in people, his wide sympathies and his accomplishments are such that he must be judged humanist *par excellence.*

Morgan writes mainly in English, although his occasional incursions into Scots show his command of the language. Snatches of dialogue in his more dramatic poems show a considerable familiarity with the Glasgow street patois. He is a highly sophisticated poet, being susceptible to a very wide range of influences and impressions. In his poems he has a curiously detached compassion engaging the feelings of the reader through the force of his argument. That quotable experiences are more numerous than quotable phrases is probably due to Morgan's intense concentration on his subject, particularly when human failure, tragedy or degradation is the theme.

From the stock-in-trade of the popular press, Morgan produces poems, many about his native Glasgow. 'King Billy' is concerned with the Protestant-Catholic troubles: 'Glasgow Green' about inborn violence in a violent city; 'The Starlings in George Square', a humorous surrealist poem about man's inhumanity to birds; 'Trio' and 'Good Friday' concerning the Christian spirit in the city (and in people everywhere).

His interest in the folk hero is manifest in the elegiacs of 'The Death of Marilyn Monroe', 'Je ne regrette rien' (in memory of Edith Piaf) and 'The Old Man and the Sea'. In his lyrics such as 'One Cigarette', 'Strawberries' and 'Absence', the transience of love, the moment of love, separation and loneliness are wistfully expressed.

E

For one who seems to reject technique for technique's sake, concrete poetry would seem to be an unlikely love. Yet Edwin Morgan declares a deep interest in this form. Much, we feel, is mere playing with words, an intellectual poet's recreational activity but in this aspect of his work we see Morgan's preoccupation with the influence of sound and word associations. From a great collection of loosely connected words and phrases in 'Message Clear', 'I am the resurrection and the life' emerges. In 'Starryveldt', from the title, conflict and violence and oppression are given forceful development.

Morgan's poetic front is ever widening and his poetry will continue to be experimental. That is the nature of the man, so observant, so sensitive to the lot of others, so committed to human causes.

Aberdeen train

Rubbing a glistening circle
on the steamed-up window I framed
a pheasant in a field of mist.
The sun was a great red thing somewhere low,
struggling with the milky scene. In the furrows
a piece of glass winked into life,
hypnotized the silly dandy; we
hooted past him with his head cocked,
contemplating a bottle-end.
And this was the last of October,
a Chinese moment in the Mearns.

from The Second Life 1968

Trio

Coming up Buchanan Street, quickly, on a sharp winter evening
a young man and two girls, under the Christmas lights –
The young man carries a new guitar in his arms,
the girl on the inside carries a very young baby,
and the girl on the outside carries a chihuahua.
And the three of them are laughing, their breath rises
in a cloud of happiness, and as they pass
the boy says, 'Wait till he sees this but!'
The chihuahua has a tiny Royal Stewart tartan coat like a teapot-
    holder,
the baby in its white shawl is all bright eyes and mouth like favours
    in a fresh sweet cake,
the guitar swells out under its milky plastic cover, tied at the neck
    with silver tinsel tape and a brisk sprig of mistletoe.
Orphean sprig! Melting baby! Warm chihuahua!
The vale of tears is powerless before you.
Whether Christ is born, or is not born, you
put paid to fate, it abdicates
                            under the Christmas lights.
Monsters of the year
go blank, are scattered back,
can't bear this march of three.

– And the three have passed, vanished in the crowd
(yet not vanished, for in their arms they wind
the life of men and beasts, and music,
laughter ringing them round like a guard)
at the end of this winter's day.

from The Second Life 1968

131

One cigarette

No smoke without you, my fire.
After you left,
your cigarette glowed on in my ashtray
and sent up a long thread of such quiet grey
I smiled to wonder who would believe its signal
of so much love. One cigarette
in the non-smoker's tray.
As the last spire
trembles up, a sudden draught
blows it winding into my face.
Is it smell, is it taste?
You are here again, and I am drunk on your tobacco lips.
Out with the light.
Let the smoke lie back in the dark.
Till I hear the very ash
sigh down among the flowers of brass
I'll breathe, and long past midnight, your last kiss.

from The Second Life 1968

In the snack-bar

A cup capsizes along the formica,
slithering with a dull clatter.
A few heads turn in the crowded evening snack-bar.
An old man is trying to get to his feet
from the low round stool fixed to the floor.
Slowly he levers himself up, his hands have no power.
He is up as far as he can get. The dismal hump
looming over him forces his head down.
He stands in his stained beltless gaberdine
like a monstrous animal caught in a tent
in some story. He sways slightly,
the face not seen, bent down
in shadow under his cap.
Even on his feet he is staring at the floor
or would be, if he could see.

I notice now his stick, once painted white
but scuffed and muddy, hanging from his right arm.
Long blind, hunchback born, half paralysed
he stands
fumbling with the stick
and speaks:
'I want – to go to the – toilet.'

It is down two flights of stairs, but we go.
I take his arm. 'Give me – your arm – it's better,' he says.
Inch by inch we drift towards the stairs.
A few yards of floor are like a landscape
to be negotiated, in the slow setting out
time has almost stopped. I concentrate
my life to his: crunch of spilt sugar,
slidy puddle from the night's umbrellas,
table edges, people's feet,
hiss of the coffee-machine, voices and laughter,
smell of a cigar, hamburgers, wet coats steaming,
and the slow dangerous inches to the stairs.
I put his right hand on the rail
and take his stick. He clings to me. The stick
is in his left hand, probing the treads.
I guide his arm and tell him the steps.
And slowly we go down. And slowly we go down.
White tiles and mirrors at last. He shambles
uncouth into the clinical gleam.
I set him in position, stand behind him
and wait with his stick.
His brooding reflection darkens the mirror
but the trickle of his water is thin and slow,
an old man's apology for living.
Painful ages to close his trousers and coat –
I do up the last buttons for him.
He asks doubtfully, 'Can I – wash my hands?'
I fill the basin, clasp his soft fingers round the soap.
He washes, feebly, patiently. There is no towel.
I press the pedal of the drier, draw his hands
gently into the roar of the hot air.
But he cannot rub them together,
drags out a handkerchief to finish.
He is glad to leave the contraption, and face the stairs.
He climbs, and steadily enough.

He climbs, we climb. He climbs
with many pauses but with that one
persisting patience of the undefeated
which is the nature of man when all is said.
And slowly we go up. And slowly we go up.
The faltering, unfaltering steps
take him at last to the door
across that endless, yet not endless waste of floor.
I watch him helped on a bus. It shudders off in the rain.
The conductor bends to hear where he wants to go.

Wherever he could go it would be dark
and yet he must trust men.
Without embarrassment or shame
he must announce his most pitiful needs
in a public place. No one sees his face.
Does he know how frightening he is in his strangeness
under his mountainous coat, his hands like wet leaves
stuck to the half-white stick?
His life depends on many who would evade him.
But he cannot reckon up the chances,
having one thing to do,
to haul his blind hump through these rains of August.
Dear Christ, to be born for this!

from The Second Life 1968

Shantyman

Shantyman, the surf of heaven
is breaking, somewhere.
White shirt in blackness,
brown arms along the rail
in the wind. And we are
plunging without stars
at midnight, singing
the sea
        to the sea.
                The sea's
ear is dull, repeat it, but
we have moved on.

All the old days are
Shenandoah.
For the present,
sing it negligent
of solemn waters and the dark.
The cutlasses won't stir,
or piles of brass and tar.

He slaps the rail, looks up
for a new verse,
we give it everything
and everything we have
rolls down to heaven like Rio
on the blue back of his hand.

from The Scotsman

Che

Even after the body
had been roughly brought
down to Vallegrande
from the hills, and the eyes
had that meaningless glaze
staring at no world,
eyes took meaning from
his slightly parted lips
showing the teeth
in a smile – no rage,
no throes, nothing
but that uncanny pro-
jection of consciousness
and a dead man putting
fate in bondage
to him. Bolivia:
what other bondages
will shiver in the cane-break
even in steel, and will break,

uniforms and proclamations
ploughed under by the very grass
itself – it rises
into the voices of forests.
For the dead wander
among its deep roots
like water, and push
the green land into heroes.
They grow in understanding,
tree, tree, man, man,
move like shadows.
Blossoms brushed
by silent bandoliers
spring out in shock and
back into place.
But jungles break.

Down from the mountains
miles and miles
a marble face,
a broken body.
The marble is only
broken by a smile.

from Bo Heem E Um (magazine)

Canedolia: *an off-concrete scotch fantasia*

oa! hoy! awe! ba! mey!

who saw?
rhu saw rum. garve saw smoo. nigg saw tain. lairg saw lagg.
rigg saw eigg. largs saw haggs. tongue saw luss. mull saw yell.
stoer saw strone. drem saw muck. gask saw noss. unst saw cults.
echt saw banff. weem saw wick. trool saw twatt.

136

how far?
from largo to lunga from joppa to skibo from ratho to shona from ulva to minto from tinto to tolsta from soutra to marsco from braco to barra from alva to stobo from fogo to fada from gigha to gogo from kelso to stroma from hirta to spango.

what is it like there?
och it's freuchie, it's faifley, it's wamphray, it's frandy, it's sliddery.

what do you do?
we foindle and fungle, we bonkle and meigle and maxpoffle. we scotstarvit, armit, wormit, and even whifflet. we play at crossstobs, leuchars, gorbals, and finfan. we scavaig, and there's aye a bit of tilquhilly. if it's wet, treshnish and mishnish.

what is the best of the country?
blinkbonny! airgold! thundergay!

and the worst?
scrishven, shiskine, scrabster, and snizort.

listen! what's that?
catacol and wauchope, never heed them.

tell us about last night
well, we had a wee ferintosh and we lay on the quiraing. it was pure strontian!

but who was there?
petermoidart and craigenkenneth and cambusputtock and ecclemuchty and corriehulish and balladolly and altnacanny and clauchanvrechan and stronachlochan and auchenlachar and tighnacrankie and tilliebruaich and killieharra and invervannach and achnatudlem and machrishellach and inchtamurchan and auchterfechan and kinlochculter and ardnawhallie and invershuggle.

and what was the toast?
schiehallion! schiehallion! schiehallion!

from The Second Life 1968

King Billy

Grey over Riddrie the clouds piled up,
dragged their rain through the cemetery trees.
The gates shone cold. Wind rose
flaring the hissing leaves, the branches
swung, heavy, across the lamps.
Gravestones huddled in drizzling shadow,
flickering streetlight scanned the requiescats,
a name and an urn, a date, a dove
picked out, lost, half regained.
What is this dripping wreath, blown from its grave
red, white, blue, and gold
'To Our Leader of Thirty Years Ago' –

Bareheaded, in dark suits, with flutes
and drums, they brought him here, in procession
seriously, King Billy of Brigton, dead,
from Bridgeton Cross: a memory of violence,
brooding days of empty bellies,
billiard smoke and a sour pint,
boots or fists, famous sherrickings,
the word, the scuffle, the flash, the shout,
bloody crumpling in the close,
bricks for papish windows, get
the Conks next time, the Conks ambush
the Billy Boys, the Billy Boys the Conks till
Sillitoe scuffs the razors down the stank –
No, but it isn't the violence they remember
but the legend of a violent man
born poor, gang-leader in the bad times
of idleness and boredom, lost in better days,
a bouncer in a betting club,
a quiet man at last, dying
alone in Bridgeton in a box bed.
So a thousand people stopped the traffic
for the hearse of a folk hero and the flutes
threw 'Onward Christian Soldiers' to the winds
from unironic lips, the mourners kept
in step, and there were some who wept.

Go from the grave. The shrill flutes
are silent, the march dispersed.
Deplore what is to be deplored,
and then find out the rest.

from The Second Life 1968

From the domain of Arnheim

And so that all these ages, these years
we cast behind us, like the smoke-clouds
dragged back into vacancy when the rocket springs –

The domain of Arnheim was all snow, but we were there.
We saw a yellow light thrown on the icefield
from the huts by the pines, and laughter came up
floating from a white corrie
miles away, clearly.
We moved on down, arm in arm.
I know you would have thought it was a dream
but we were there. And those were trumpets –
tremendous round the rocks –
while they were burning fires of trash and mammoths' bones.
They sang naked, and kissed in the smoke.
A child, or one of their animals, was crying.
Young men blew the ice crystals off their drums.
We came down among them, but of course
they could see nothing, on their time-scale.
Yet they sensed us, stopped, looked up – even into our eyes.
To them we were a displacement of the air,
a sudden chill, yet we had no power
over their fear. If one of them had been dying
he would have died. The crying
came from one just born: that was the cause
of the song. We saw it now. What had we stopped
but joy?
I know you felt
the same dismay, you gripped my arm, they were waiting
for what they knew of us to pass.

A sweating trumpeter took
a brand from the fire with a shout and threw it
where our bodies would have been –
we felt nothing but his courage.
And so they would deal with every imagined power
seen or unseen.
There are no gods in the domain of Arnheim.

We signalled to the ship; got back;
our lives and days returned to us, but
haunted by deeper souvenirs than any rocks or seeds.
From time the souvenirs are deeds.

from The Second Life 1968

Alexander Scott

Alexander Scott was born in Aberdeen in 1920 and took an honours degree in English at Aberdeen University. He served in the Second World War in the Gordon Highlanders in France, the Low Countries and in Normandy, was wounded at Reichswald and won the M.C. Since 1948 he has lectured in Scottish Literature at Glasgow University, and he is now head of the new Department of Scottish Literature. He has written a number of works of scholarship, notably *Still Life* 1958, a critical biography of William Soutar, as well as essays, articles and reviews for scholarly periodicals and journalism of a high order. As founder-editor of *The Saltire Review* (1954-57), he laid the foundations for many subsequent periodicals.

Though first and foremost a poet, Alexander Scott has written a number of plays for stage and radio, and short stories. His earliest volume of poems *The Latest in Elegies* appeared in 1949 and was followed by *Selected Poems* 1950 and *Mouth Music* 1954 but it was not until the broadcast of his television poem on Aberdeen, 'Heart of Stone' 1966, a fine poem in which he views his native city without rose-coloured spectacles, and the publication of *Cantrips* 1968, that he became known to a wider public.

Cantrips, despite its title, is not all frolic and fun, for Scott is a poet with serious purpose. Yet he obviously rhymes for fun. Muscularity and gusto characterise most of his work, but when in some of his lyrics he deviates into tenderness, the reader is pleasantly surprised.

A large part of his work is satirical and there we see his goliardic manner in which he delights himself and also his readers, using the metres, rhythms and alliteration of the Makars. His cryptic 'Doun wi' Dirt', 'Paradise Tint', 'Lit. Crit.' and his 'Aphorisms' are most stimulating.

From the derisively comic to the deadly serious, Alexander Scott is an important verse commentator of our times. His forceful verse would at times be somewhat hectoring were it not for the inevitable intrusion of humour. His extravagance of expression is a pleasing additive to his work. The richness of his own Aberdeen vocabulary comes from a true son of that City who has a well-stored literary mind. The judicious mingling of slang with Aberdeen words enhances the comic effect of his poems.

Robustness and clarity and directness have characterised most of Alexander Scott's poetry up to the present, although a tender personal note, seen more generally in his English poems, has been appearing more frequently, and the combination of these moods gives Scott's work its characteristic appeal and virtuosity.

Haar in Princes Street

The heicht o the biggins is happit in rauchens o haar,
    The statues alane
     Stand clearly, heid til fit in stane,
And lour frae *then* and *thonder* at *hencefurth* and *here*.

The past on pedestals, girnan frae ilka feature,
    Wi granite frouns
     They glower on the present's feckless loons,
Its gangrels tint i the haar that fankles the future.

The fowk o flesh, stravaigan wha kens whither,
    And come frae whaur,
     Hudder like ghaists i the gastrous haar,
Forfochten and wae i the smochteran smore o the weather

They swaiver and flirn i the freeth like straes i the sea,
    An airtless swither,
     Steeran awa the t'ane frae t'ither,
Alane, and lawlie aye to be lanesome sae.

haar mist   *heicht* height, top   *biggins* buildings   *happit* clothed
rauchens mantles, clouds   *lour* look sullenly   *girnan* grimacing, grumbling
ilka every   *glower* glare   *feckless* feeble   *loons* fellows
gangrels unsteady children   *tint* lost   *fankles* entangles
stravaigan wandering   *gastrous* monstrous   *forfochten* worn out   *wae* sad
smore suffocation   *flirn* twist   *freeth* foam, froth   *lawlie* reluctant

But heich i the lift (whaur the haar is skailan fairlie
    In blufferts o wind)
And blacker nor nicht whan starns are blind,
The Castle looms – a fell, a fabulous ferlie.

Dragonish, darksome, dourlie grapplan the Rock
    Wi claws o stane
That scart our history bare til the bane,
It braks like Fate throu Time's wanchancy reek.

from The Latest in Elegies 1949

Calvinist sang

A hunder pipers canna blaw
    Our trauchled times awa,
Drams canna droun them out, nor sang
Hap their scarecraw heids for lang.

Gin aa the warld was bleezan fou,
    Whit gowk wad steer the plou?
Gin chiels were cowpan quines aa day,
They'd mak (but miss at gaitheran) hay.

Pit by your bagpipes, brak your gless,
    Wi quines, keep aff the gress,
The-day ye need a hert and harns
As dour as the diamant, cauld as the starns.

from The Latest in Elegies 1949

lift sky	*skailan* spilling	*fell* terrible	
ferlie wonder	*scart* scratch	*wanchancy* unlucky	
trauchled troubled	*drams* drinks of whisky		*gin* if
bleezan fighting	*gowk* fool	*chiels* fellows	
cowpan seducing	*quines* lasses	*the-day* today	
harns brains	*dour* unyielding	*starns* stars	

The sodgers

Nae wi the gallus captains
That never jinkit war
But socht for glory's wildfire lowe
As wise men aince for anither star –

And nae wi the ramstam colonels
That leuch at the din o the drum
And skirled for the bleeze o battle's Inferno
As saunts micht skirl for Kingdom Come –

But aye wi the sweirt sodgers
That never wished to dee
And only marched thon *forrard* road
Sen onie *back* they couldna see –

Near blind wi the reek o wappins
And the reek o leean words,
But never near sae blind wi bluid
As faa in love wi guns and swords.

from The Latest in Elegies 1949

Lethe

Gin the Water o Leith was the Water o Lethe,
Hou deep wad I drink o its dozent flume?
Hou deep wad I droun in its drumlie lapper?
Hou deep wad I dee in its thowless doom?

But the Water o Leith frae the Water o Lethe
Is fremmit and far as the fact frae the dream—
Their burns wad as sune gae mellan thegither
As sparks frae a spunk wi the levin's leam.

gallus foolhardy	*jinkit* dodged	*lowe* light	*ramstam* impulsive
sweirt reluctant	*wappins* weapons		*leean* lying
dozent drowsy, slow moving	*flume* current		*drumlie* thick, gloomy
lapper wave	*thowless* spiritless		*fremmit* foreign
mellan mingling	*spunk* match	*levin's leam* lightning's flash

Gin the Water o Leith was the Water o Lethe,
I never wad sup ae bebble ava,
For wha wad mind o the life I connached
Gin I forgot i the sweelan swaw?

I' the Water o Leith (as the Water o Lethe)
I'd neither drink nor droun nor dee,
But turn frae its wanhope awa til the warld
And leave it alane to get tint i the sea.

from Selected Poems 1950

Senses

The beast in its earth ablow me,
The bird i the lift abune,
Hae aa their senses lively
To watch the warld gae roun.

But here I walk atween them
Wi dazzle-darkened een
And lugs that the rair o the city
Has deaved to simple soun.

I walk in a warld atween them
Wi theirs outside my ken,
A kind o stravaigan statue
Wi harns in a heid o stane.

from Mouth Music 1954

connached wasted   *sweelan* whirling
swaw agitation of surface   *wanhope* despair   *tint* lost
lugs ears   *deaved* deafened
stravaigan aimlessly wandering   *harns* brains

Great eneuch

Gin I was great eneuch, thon naukit tree
Wad bleeze its lane in beauty's lowe for me,
To fleer the wae o winter out o my een
And mak a Mey o Mairch, a glamour lee
Mair true nor truth to tell what truth micht mean,
      Gin I was great eneuch.

Gin I was great eneuch, my shilpit hert
Wad brier sae braid as rive my breist apairt
And tak the yirth for flesh, the sea for bluid,
Till aa was kent – the tirl o ilka airt,
O' ilka tide – and aa was kent as guid,
      Gin I was great eneuch.

But I'm no great eneuch, and sae my lack
Maun serve, for gin my hert has little knack
For hauddan the warld's rowth, and gin my sicht
Just glisks on beauty, still there's sangs to mak
That nocht but loss alane can sing aricht
      (Gin loss be great eneuch).

And loss is great eneuch that wants the haill
(Aa life, aa space, aa time) and aye maun fail
To win thon prize, yet canna cease to sing
The strivin for 't o ilka separate sel, –
And siccan sangs frae my ain lack I'd wring,
      Gin I was great eneuch.

from Mouth Music 1954

eneuch enough	*gin* if	*naukit* naked	*lane* own
lowe light	*fleer* banish	*shilpit* feeble	*brier* grow
yirth earth	*tirl* vibration	*airt* direction of the wind	
knack skill	*rowth* plenty	*glisks* glances	
aricht rightly	*sel* self-being	*siccan* such	

146

I spak wi the spaewife

I spak wi the spaewife, speiran cauldrife questions,
And she gied back to me her snorlit answers,
And aye frae the crystal, set on the stane atween us,
I glowered awa, but still I saw its pictures.

Twa images thonder mellit to mak a ferlie
(As amber gless micht sink in amber water
Till twa looked ane, and yet were twa for aa that,
The sunlicht strikkan baith wi a different glister) –

The t'ane: – a hawk that hung i the brou o heaven
On wings sae swith to tirl they seemed to stand,
The wheel o the warld sic deeps o faa ablow him
Shrunk til a nest to stoop on, rive, and wound;

The t'ither: – a laverock, tashed wi grumly talons
And dunted doun on the yirth to dee i the stour,
Her breist a sotter o bluid, but wings aye reemlan
To spire frae the death that limed the livan air.

And yet, and yet – they mirlit, the t'ane in t'ither
(The amber flume aneth the amber gless
And ower it syne, a faa and lift o lappers)
Till truth was tint in a swither that looked like lees.

For whiles it seemed the hawk whas pouerless pinions
Sklintered in stour, or the laverock raise frae death
On kelteran wings that heezed her kaiser o heaven,
And whiles they mellit sae close, I tint them baith.

The crystal stuid on the stane atween the twa o's
And opened afore my een the twa o'ts picturs,
And aye I speired at the spaewife cauldrife questions,
And aye she gied me back her snorlit answers.

from Mouth Music 1954

spaewife fortune teller   *cauldrife* chill   *snorlit* confusing (ambiguous)
mellit mingled   *ferlie* wonderful vision   *t'ane* one   *swith* swift
tirl vibrate   *laverock* lark   *tashed* stained   *grumly* grim
dunted struck   *yirth* earth   *sotter* mass   *reemlan* trembling   *spire* soar
limed caught   *mirlit* melted   *aneth* beneath   *swither* aimless movement
lappers waves   *sklintered* splintered   *kelteran* swift beating   *kaiser* emperor

Paradise tint

Said Adam til Eve,
'Ye've gart me grieve.'
Said Eve til Adam,
'Aipples, I've had 'em!'

Said Adam til Nick,
'Ye snake! Ye swick!'
Said Nick til Adam,
'Me – or the madam?'

Said Adam til 's sel,
'A wumman 's hell.'
Said 's sel til Adam,
'Doubled, ye'd wad 'em.'

Said Adam til God,
'What wey sae odd?'
Said God til Adam,
'Never ye'll faddom.'   *from Cantrips 1968*

Science fiction

Escaped to the stars,
Gone rocketting out in the black dazzle of space,
Wrenched up from history, how he steers
For the future's vast, the void's peace.

But the void roars,
The future swims into time on the blood's wave,
Wherever and ever the rocket careers,
It cargoes history's homespun weave.

His freedom a ghost
He hunts in a forest of suns, a phantom quest,
He must have glimpsed it flee, and guessed
His heart could fill the hugest waste?

from Mouth Music 1954

tint lost	*gart* made	*Nick* the Devil
swick cheat	*wad* wed	

Big beat

A sair stramash – a hairse wee quinie quavers
On hauflin love, her sang a wheen o havers;

A bourach o hardly-happit jigtime burdies
Gae yokan barebuff wames til a yark o hurdies;

Three babbity blondes, three pooter-doos, are cooan,
Their shiel a rickle o chords in rowters' ruin;

A gastrous fraik, his phizz as grim as gorgon,
Maks lownderan love til a less-nor-michty organ;

A bonnie bucko, gifted (by God?) til tumphies,
Stounds like a stirk, and back they grain like grumphies;

A spanky spade lats lowse as heich a yammer
As tines aa sense (langsyne he tint aa grammar);

And loud or laich, but deavan aye the lughole,
The gueetars gowp like watter doun the plughole –

O wash awa this weird! O sain this passion!
This pyne o youth that stangs wi sair stramashin!

from Cantrips 1968

sair sorry, great   stramash tumult, row   hairse hoarse
quinie lassie   hauflin adolescent
wheen o havers lot of nonsense   bourach group, cluster
hardly happit scantily clothed   burdies lasses   yokan twisting
yark jerk   hurdies bottoms   babbity infant
pooter doos pouter pigeons   shiel shelter, refuge
rickle a loose heap   rowters' bellowers'   gastrous ghastly
fraik freak   phizz face   lownderan noisy beating
bucko fellow   tumphies dullards   stounds roars
grumphies pigs   spanky frisky   spade negro
heich high pitched   yammer yell of distress   tines loses
langsyne long before   deavan deafening   gowp gulp
weird fate   sain cleanse, heal   stangs stings

149

Doun wi dirt!

'De Sade?'
'Ach, gyaad!'

'Masoch?'
'Eh, fyauch!'

'Frank Harris?'
'Guid war us!'

'Jim Joyce?'
'Nae choice!'

'Bert Lawrence?'
'Abhorrrrence!'

'Hank Miller?'
'Wud spiller!'

'Jean Genet?'
'Och, dinnae!'

'Bill Burroughs?'
'Gomorrah's!'

'Syd Smith?'
'Deil's kith!'

'Al Trocchi?'
'Fell mochie!'

'Al Sharp?'
'Coorse carp!'

'The bourach?'
'Just smoorich!'

'Mankind?'   *from Cantrips 1968*
'Muck-mind!'

'And you?'
'Weel, nou – '

wud mad
spiller spoiler
bourach crowd, the set
smoorich a big wet kiss

Cry

Breakdown, breakdown, lay me low,
I'll go where all the furies go,
Into my own Orestian heart,
And tear it apart, tear it apart.

Breakdown, breakdown, hoist me high,
I'll fly where all the vultures fly,
Into my own Orphean brain,
And pick it clean, pick it clean.

Breakdown, breakdown, drive me deep,
I'll creep where all the blindworms creep,
Into my own Tiresian blood,
And drink its flood, drink its flood.

Breakdown, breakdown, pay me peace,
I'll cease where all the madmen cease,
Inside my own Oedipan mind,
And brand it blind, brand it blind.

from Scottish Poetry 4 1969

Domestic bliss
Or nothing personal

Bide on your back, ye bauchlie limmer,
   Bide in your bed and dee!
Owre lang your feet hae trailed the causeys,
   Lang they hae trampled me,
But nou ye're doun by the guff o the graveyaird
   And I'm abune ye, hie!

Be still, ye jaud, that were aye steeran,
   Stiller nor still ye'll lie,
Be quate, ye tongue that deaved me dirlan
   Wi clapperan clash and cry,
For aa your aiths, your fleerin and flytin,
   Death winna fleg doun-by.

It's him maun wad ye, him maun wale ye
   To sleep in 's bed o stane,
And me ye merried, ye'll mak me single,
   A haill new life to hain,
Wi ilka day to bless your deein,
   And ilka nicht my lane.

from Akros No. 15 1970

bauchlie clumsy	*limmer* jade	*bide* remain
owre too *causeys* streets		*abune* above
steerin bustling about	*deaved* deafened	
fleerin grousing	*fleg* be scared	*maun* must
wale choose	*hain* cherish	*lane* self

152

Von Braun

You built the *Apollos*
from London bones.

Your hypodermic stabbed space
and drew blood.

Was Cain the captain
who read us *Genesis* round the moon?

Killing creator,
breath to a dead world.

Whose bones will we bury
to grace it green?

from Scottish Poetry 5 1970

Revolution

Be brithers
– Or smithers.

not previously published

Scotch education

I tellt ye
I tellt ye.

from Scottish Poetry 5 1970

George Mackay Brown

George Mackay Brown's first volume of poems, *The Storm and other Poems* 1954, has as its title poem 'The Storm', a symbolic poem in which the poet, going to sea in rough weather, is buffeted and tossed about, his boat dismasted and he himself cast ashore.

> I tell you this my son: after
> That God sent storm, I find peace here
> These many years with
> The Grey Monks of Eynhallow.

Here emerged a poet with a future.

As poet of Orkney, George Mackay Brown follows Edwin Muir. Born in 1921, the son of a tailor and postman in Stromness, he was educated at Stromness Academy. It is significant that Browns have lived in these parts for four hundred years. From an early age, he was writing poetry but it was not until he spent a year in 1951-52 at Newbattle Abbey College, Midlothian, under Edwin Muir that his literary powers truly blossomed. He then took an honours degree at Edinburgh University. Since then he has lived in, and generally written about Orkney.

Like Muir, Mackay Brown is a religious poet but there the resemblance ends. While Muir was driven early from his Eden, and experienced squalor, misery and degradation in Glasgow, George Mackay Brown has maintained a steady course and only left Orkney for the few years of his academic studies. He is deeply interested in humanity but confines his creative activity mainly to writing about Orkney people and their Norse forbears. If his range in space is narrow, in time it is enormous for while Muir concerned himself with man in his modern environment, George Mackay Brown looks at people involved with the elements, in a historical context. Nature for him is red in tooth and claw but the storm and adversity in general are 'Godsent' and an essential part of human existence. The victims nevertheless enlist the poet's pity.

George Mackay Brown is constantly searching for order in human life. He found it for himself in the Roman Catholic Church in 1961. From his earliest writings ritual, custom and such links between today and eternity are, to the poet, permanent elements in ever-changing existence. In the settled Orkney communities, men and women stoically maintain the age-old customs of birth, marriage and death, as they gain hard-earned livelihood between fertile fields and the sea where tragedy is never far away. The poet shares many of the experiences of the people about whom he writes and a delightful tolerance and humour infuses his writing.

The symbolic title of his second volume *Loaves and Fishes* 1959 signifies the poet's involvement with sea, land and Christianity. The division of the volume into three parts, (1) The Drowning Wave (2) Crofts along the Shore and (3) The Redeeming Wave, indicate the increasing comprehensiveness of the poet's work. The harvest of silver (fish) and gold (corn), the toll exacted by the sea, the pierhead yarn, calm religious contemplation of Eynhallow are all there. All life is important to this poet. In *The Year of the Whale* 1965, the poet's third volume, the poetic harvest is even more ample.

George Mackay Brown in addition to writing poetry has exploited his remarkable gift for narrative in two volumes of short stories: A *Calendar of Love* 1967 and *A Time to Keep* 1969. The many delightful stories are full of the poetry of the poems. For those who find the complexity of the poems difficult (the influence of the Metaphysicals and Gerard Manley Hopkins is apparent), the short stories are a happy substitute. George Mackay Brown has also written a successful play, *A Spell for Green Corn* 1970.

Perhaps his guide to Orkney, *An Orkney Tapestry* 1969, is the best introduction to the Islands and to the work of George Mackay Brown. While in his *An Autobiography* Edwin Muir concentrates on the fable, George Mackay Brown, with no less deep insight, provides the story with a key to the understanding of Orkney and himself.

Unlucky boat

That boat has killed three people. Building her
Sib drove a nail through his thumb. He died in his croft
Bunged to the eyes with rust and penicillin.
One evening when the Flow was a bar of silver
Under the moon, and Mansie and Tom with wands
Were putting a spell on cuithes, she dipped a bow
And ushered Mansie, his pipe still in his teeth,
To meet the cold green angels. They hauled her up
Among the rocks, right in the path of Angus,
Whose neck, rigid with pints from the Dounby Market,
Snapped like a barley stalk. . . . There she lies,
A leprous unlucky bitch, in the quarry of Moan.

Tinkers, going past, make the sign of the cross.

from Honour'd Shade 1959

  cuithes coal fish

Our Lady of the waves

The twenty brothers of Eynhallow
Have made a figure of Our Lady.
From red stone they carved her
And set her on a headland.
There spindrift salts her feet.
At dawn the brothers sang this
    Blessed Lady, since midnight
    We have done three things
    We have bent hooks.
    We have patched a sail.
    We have sharpened knives.
    Yet the little silver brothers are afraid.
    Bid them come to our net.
    Show them our fire, our fine round plates.
    Per Dominum Christum nostrum
    Look mildly on our hungers.

The codling hang in a row by the wall.
At noon the brothers sang this
    Holy Mother, Una the cow
    Gives thin blue milk.
    Where is the golden thread of butter?
    The stone in the middle of our glebe
    Has deep black roots.
    We have broken three ploughs on it.
    Per Christum Dominum nostrum
    Save Una from the axe,
    Our dappled cow with large eyes.

The girls go by with pails to the byre.
At sunset the brothers sang this
    Sweet Virgin, the woman of Garth
    Is forever winking at Brother Paul.
    She puts an egg in his palm.
    She lays peats in his cowl.
    Her neck is long as spilt milk.
    Brother Paul is a good lad.
    Well he carries word and wine for the priest.
    But three red midnights
    His tongue has run loose among dreams.

Paul has broken knees at the stone.
At midnight the brothers sang this
    Queen of Heaven, this good day
    There is a new cradle at Quoys.
    It rocks on the blue floor.
    And there is a new coffin at Hamnavoe.
    Arnor the poet lies there
    Tired of words and wounds.
    In between, what is man?
    A head bent over fish and bread and ale.
    Outside, the long furrow.
    Through a door, a board with a shape on it.

Guard the plough and the nets.

Star of the sea shine for us.

from The Year of the Whale 1965

Old fisherman with guitar

A formal exercise for withered fingers.
   The head is bent,
     The eyes half closed, the tune
Lingers
     And beats, a gentle wing the west had thrown
Against his breakwater wall with salt savage lament.

So fierce and sweet the song on the plucked string,
   Know now for truth
     Those hands have cut from the net
The strong
     Crab-eaten corpse of Jock washed from a boat
One old winter, and gathered the mouth of Thora to his
     mouth.

from The Year of the Whale 1965

Hamnavoe Market

They drove to the Market with ringing pockets.

Folster found a girl
Who put wounds on his face and throat,
Small and diagonal, like red doves.

Johnston stood beside the barrel.
All day he stood there.
He woke in a ditch, his mouth full of ashes.

Grieve bought a balloon and a goldfish.
He swung through the air.
He fired shotguns, rolled pennies, ate sweet fog from a stick.

Heddle was at the Market also.
I know nothing of his activities.
He is and always was a quiet man.

Garson fought three rounds with a negro boxer,
And received thirty shillings,
Much applause, and an eye loaded with thunder.

Where did they find Flett?
They found him in a brazen circle,
All flame and blood, a new Salvationist.

A gypsy saw in the hand of Halcro
Great strolling herds, harvests, a proud woman.
He wintered in the poorhouse.

They drove home from the Market under the stars
Except for Johnston
Who lay in a ditch, his mouth full of dying fires.

from The Year of the Whale 1965

Snow: from a hospital

1

Best leave the paper blank.
If you *must* write,
Imitate old smiling Chinamen.
They scribbled on silk,
Three arrows in a corner (trees),
A broken diagonal,
And February's dyke is full.

2

This is the snow for me –
My bronchial tree loaded and loud
With the white birds of winter.

3

They come from Venus, Orion, Betelgeuse,
Such unearthly cargoes!
Now wrecked here,
The innumerable shining bales are too much.
What can we do with such delicacy?
Our coarse eyes long for grass, stone, puddle.

4

Winds like the hands of Penelope
Forever weave
Web after web of snow.
When will Odysseus come, the golden hero?
After the ploughman, sower, harrower.

5

This snow is like time in its youth.
Against that light
Tinkers are blacker and fiercer,
Birds hungrier,
What so bright as apples and stars and children!
But the swan is jealous.
She pushes her dingy breast over the loch
To find some blue.

6

How clumsy and endearing he is,
The snowman,
A flocculent teddy bear.
But I tell you, friends,
He's not what he seems to be.
This February
His claws tore my chest open.

from Scottish Poetry 3 1968

The heavenly stones

Three men came to our door with gifts
When I was a lightsome lad.
Yellow and red and black they stood
Against the milking shed.

'Will you take the sign of wealth?' said one
And gave me a disc of gold,
The same with which God's corn and wine
Are dearly bought and sold.

I ran with it to the midden heap
And sank it in that filth.
'If that's how you treat good gold,' laughed he,
'You lock the door on wealth.'

The red one said, 'My jar's sweet fume
Is sensuality.'
What sound was that? My father's boar
Rutting behind the stye.

I tilted the vessel with my foot
Till the dark oil shimmered out.
'If that's how you treat the dancing five,
Go wear a beggar's clout;

'Who might have had heraldic cloaks
Over your shoulder slung,
And bedded with more beautiful girls
Than ever Solomon sung.'

The third old man came shuffling up
And opened his earthen bottle:
'O what are breast and thigh but dust,
And what is yellow metal?

'Taste the bitters in my cruse,
Nor twist your face, my son.
This has grown on the tree of life
Since Adam's day began.

'And you must hang on your tree
Watered with women's tears,
The grape of God that ripens slow
Through forty hundred years.

'The men of dust will pluck you down
And eat your flesh for food,
And angel fingered, fill their flasks
At the five gates of your blood.

'Drink this wine now, that you may know
What Adam had to suffer,
And what atonement, on that day,
A son of God must offer.'. . .

I longed to spit it from my mouth
But yet I drank it down
With anguish, and the three old men
Rode onward to the town.

That hour I felt mortality
Fasten about my bones.
The gold out of the midden sang
And heaven leaked from the stones.

The shaken branch, The Voice, the draped
Whispering coil of flame,
And Eve, a tall unfingered harp
Strung with desire and shame.

All the world's honey and its dust
Through my five senses falling . . .
Till from the hearth stone where she knelt
I heard my mother calling,

And heard my father's restless saw
Rasping through the wood –
Old craftsman, making crib and cross
Where simple trees had stood.

A Roman column under the moon
Passed like a gleaming wave
That time would scatter, each bright drop
To its salt separate grave.

I flung away the heavenly stones
Yellow and black and red
That I had played with all day long,
And, laughing, crept to bed.

from Loaves and Fishes 1959

The hawk

On Sunday the hawk fell on Bigging
    And a chicken screamed
    Lost in its own little snowstorm.
And on Monday he fell on the moor
    And the Field Club
    Raised a hundred silent prisms.
And on Tuesday he fell on the hill
    And the happy lamb
    Never knew why the loud collie straddled him.
And on Wednesday he fell on a bush
    And the blackbird
    Laid by his little flute for the last time.
And on Thursday he fell on Cleat
    And peerie Tom's rabbit
    Swung in a single arc from shore to hill.
And on Friday he fell on a ditch
    But the rampant rat,
    That eye and that tooth, quenched his flame.
And on Saturday he fell on Bigging
    And Jock lowered his gun
    And nailed a small wing over the corn.

from The Year of the Whale 1965

peerie small

Country girl

I make seven circles, my love
For your good breaking.
I make the gray circle of bread
And the circle of ale
And I drive the butter round in a golden ring
And I dance when you fiddle
And I turn my face with the turning sun till your
   feet come in from the field.
My lamp throws a circle of light,
Then you lie for an hour in the hot unbroken
   circle of my arms.

from The Year of the Whale 1965

Haddock fishermen

Midnight. The wind yawing nor-east.
A low blunt moon.
Unquiet beside quiet wives we rest.

A spit of rain and a gull
In the open door.
The lit fire. A quick mouthful of ale.

We push the *Merle* at a sea of cold flame.
The oars drip honey.
Hook by hook uncoils under The Kame.

Our line breaks the trek of sudden thousands.
Twelve nobbled jaws,
Gray cowls, gape in our hands,

Twelve cold mouths scream without sound.
The sea is empty again.
Like tinkers the bright ones endlessly shift
                    their ground.

We probe emptiness all the afternoon;
Unyoke: and taste
The true earth-food, beef and a barley scone.

Sunset drives a butcher blade
In the day's throat.
We turn through an ebb salt and sticky
                                    as blood.

More stars than fish. Women, cats, a gull
Mewl at the rock.
The valley divides the meagre miracle.

from Fishermen with Ploughs (1971)

Winter bride

The three fishermen said to Jess of The Shore
'A wave took Jock
Between The Kist and The Sneuk.
We couldn't get him, however we placed the boat.
With all that drag and clutch and swell
He has maybe one in a hundred chances'
They left some mouthing cuithes in the door.
She had stood in this threshold, fire and innocence,
A winter bride.
Now she laid off her workaday shawl.
She put on the black.
(Girl and widow across a drowned wife
Laid wondering neck on neck.)
She took the soundless choir of fish
And a sharp knife
And went the hundred steps to the pool in the rock.
Give us this day our daily bread
She swilled and cut
And laid psalms and blessings on her dish.

In the bay the waves pursued their indifferent dances.

from Fishermen with Ploughs (1971)

cuithes coal fish

165

Warped boat

As one would say, lighting an evening pipe
At a banked fire,
'Barley will soon be ripe.
Ale should be sweet in the Mouth this year
With all that rain in May, though the seedtime
                                        was dry.' . . .
So Willag, before the *Merle* turned over
Rose from the rowlocks
And remarked to the open mouths on the shore,
'Drive old Bess, that fence-breaker, from the
                                        oats
Back to her patch of clover.
Yes, Breck can have my horse for his five goats.
And Jeannie is wrong again.
She raged by all that was holy I'd drown and
                                        die
In steepings of malt.
A fine evening it was for going to the sillocks.
But men,
It's a coarse drink at the end of a day, this
                                        salt!
His sea boots filled, and Willag said no more.

from Fishermen with Ploughs (1971)

sillocks small coal fish easily caught in large numbers with
unbaited hooks

Iain Crichton Smith

Born in Lewis in 1928, Iain Crichton Smith grew up in a community where Gaelic rather than English was spoken and thought. After taking a degree in English at Aberdeen University, he became a schoolmaster and for some years now has taught English at Oban High School, meantime writing a number of volumes of poetry. He writes with equal fluency both poetry and prose in Gaelic and English although most of his published work is in English as it provides readier publication and a greater readership. Recently he has published a masterly verse translation of Duncan Ban Macintyre's *In Praise of Ben Dorain* 1969 and two novels, *Consider the Lilies* 1968, about an old Highland woman's experience of the Sutherland clearances and *The Last Summer* 1969, about a sixteen-year-old lad in the Highlands, a volume of short stories, *Survival without Error* 1970, and a considerable number of short stories in Gaelic and English together with some plays and critical writing on Gaelic and Scottish literature.

In his writing his own inherited residue from Calvinism and his humanitarianism are in conflict and he struggles to reconcile opposing elements. He is everywhere concerned with the individual's isolation from other beings in his world of metaphors, unable to see beyond them what is actually there. Iain Crichton Smith expresses deep compassion for members of the human kind so ingloriously trapped within their worlds of conflict and illusion and disillusion. The poet realises somewhat ruefully the poet's exceptional sensitivity to, and keener awareness of, distress and loneliness.

Iain Crichton Smith draws on the natural scene of his own Hebrides and Highlands for inspiration but it is the nature of people that concerns him. Not for him, he says, the poetry of statement but rather a poetry which contains fighting tensions. He has the gift of sustained poetry and has written in English and Gaelic long poems in poetic sequences. Notable is 'Deer on the High Hills' where he

167

explores the theme of man's isolation from other things. In a series of striking similes and metaphors, he gives the deer an independent life. He refers to the dualism of Duncan Ban Macintyre's love for the deer yet his shooting of them. The deer are a 'world away' from us humans.

The titles of his two most considerable volumes, *Thistles and Roses* 1961 and *The Law and the Grace* 1965 indicate his preoccupation with the conflict in himself of the world of inhibitions, constraints and endurance alongside the desire for 'the unscented rose he grows in his heart's south.'

In Iain Crichton Smith's latest volume, *From Bourgeois Land* 1969 a sequence of thirty-nine poems, he is moving into the wider field of world affairs when he shows his disturbance at the effects on people of urbanisation, commercialisation, war and the absence of purpose of life in the city. For the poet apathy and bloody-mindedness (in its old sense) go together resulting in cruel authoritarian rule and Belsen-like atrocities.

Features of Iain Crichton Smith's poetic style are the employment of a conversational approach even in his most complex poems. There are the cadences of his native Gaelic, with the limpid rise and fall of language across the ends of lines, the prominence of the strong conjunction 'and' giving the poems a certain rhetorical force as image upon image builds up. There is a compression of language, an incisiveness. He does not go in for free verse, preferring a restricting structure, a 'cage', as he expresses it, in which to work.

Iain Crichton Smith is not the poet to stand still, but continues to develop. His two novels, published after he was forty, show that. In his newer role as a social commentator and critic, he seems to be altering direction as yet somewhat tentatively. Recently his new modernity and interest in the wider world has manifested itself in his volume of short stories.

Some days were running legs

Some days were running legs and joy
and old men telling tomorrow would be
a fine day surely: for sky was red
at setting of sun between the hills.

Some nights were parting at the gates
with day's companions: and dew falling
on heads clear of ambition except light
returning and throwing stones at sticks.

Some days were rain flooding forever the green
pasture: and horses turning to the wind
bare smooth backs. The toothed rocks rising
sharp and grey out of the ancient sea.

Some nights were shawling mirrors lest the lightning
strike with eel's speed out of the storm.
Black the roman rooks came from the left squawking
and the evening flowed back around their wings.

from The Long River 1955

Poem of Lewis

Here they have no time for the fine graces
of poetry, unless it freely grows
in deep compulsion, like water in the well,
woven into the texture of the soil
in a strong pattern. They have no rhymes
to tailor the material of thought
and snap the thread quickly on the tooth.
One would have thought that this black north
was used to lightning, crossing the sky like fish
swift in their element. One would have thought
the barren rock would give a value to
the bursting flower. The two extremes,
mourning and gaiety, meet like north and south
in the one breast, milked by knuckled time,
till dryness spreads across each aging bone.

They have no place for the fine graces
of poetry. The great forgiving spirit of the word
fanning its rainbow wing, like a shot bird
falls from the windy sky. The sea heaves
in visionless anger over the cramped graves
and the early daffodil, purer than a soul,
is gathered into the terrible mouth of the gale.

from The Long River 1955

In Luss churchyard

Light strikes the stone bible like a gong:
blank leaves gape open. Greenness of grass is most
what, raging round the slabs, astonishes
the casual visitor drifting like a ghost
among the inscriptions and the wishes
chiselled on stone, prayed for a dead tongue.

A bird flickers from bough to windless bough
unsettled, frenzied perhaps with heat
or violence of the breast, a pagan joy.
The stranger remarks anew his moving feet
so constantly labouring in his employ
and walking without thought as they do now:

and the very inscriptions mirror modes of death –
the early stately and the later terse
(the very early almost invisible).
Consider how this eighteenth-century verse
glides with a quiet charm through pastoral
landscapes of the wandering breath.

Here however a skull, there crossed bones
leap out with tigerish instancy, like fire
burning through paper: with a savage force
punch through electric noon where the hands perspire
and prickle with the sun. This is indeed a coarse
imagery to be carved on harmless stones.

The adjacent river rambles quietly on
with wayward music, hardly disturbing even
the image of a leaf or stone or stick
but holding all the amplitude of heaven –
the fiery blueness of a composed Atlantic –
arching an earth poised in the breathless noon

where living and dead turn on the one hinge
of a noon intensely white, intensely clear.
The eyes read dates: the hands steady and rest
on leaning stone without a twitch of fear
merely an aimless curiosity. The breast,
empty with indifference, broods in change.

Yet, should a charge populous, terrible,
burst through the feeding greenness, capsizing this
mound like a knotted table, knees would sink
into the imponderable abyss
where the one star burns with a convulsive wink
in a white sky, blown outwards like a bubble.

The silence holds. A saw nags at a tree.
The settled bird chirps briefly while a breeze
ruffles its breast. The eye confused by dates
is pleasurably excited by the trees
arching a coolness over the heavy gates.
Therefore out of the noon's implacable sea

of hammered light the feet, still steady, go.
The hands touch wood and push the gate away
from the dreaming body which casts a little shade.
Out of the hectic greenness into a day
of dusty roadways the feet, suddenly gripping, wade
gathering power, changing to swift from slow.

from New Poets 1959

John Knox

That scything wind has cut the rich corn down –
the satin shades of France spin idly by –
the bells are jangled in St Andrew's town –
a thunderous God tolls from a northern sky.
He pulls the clouds like bandages awry.
See how the harlot bleeds below her crown.
This lightning stabs her in the heaving thigh –
such siege is deadly for her dallying gown.

A peasant's scythe rings churchbells from the stone.
From this harsh battle let the sweet birds fly,
surprised by fields, now barren of their corn.
(Invent, bright friends, theology or die.)
The shearing naked absolute blade has torn
through false French roses to her foreign cry.

from Thistles and Roses 1961

from 'Seagulls'

There is nothing anyone can do with these
sheer naked wills that dominate this sea.
Nearer to stone
than to a thinking man
they have no cruel look or kind. Amuse
yourself with fantasies, these will not come
out of the different air which is their home.
Your circles cannot touch. No tangent may
even lightly curve through blue to join you to
a seagull's world which at the centre is
the single-headed seagull in the blue
image you make for it, its avarice
its only passion that is really true.
You cannot admire it even. It is simply
a force that, like a bomb slim as a death,
plunges, itself, no other, through the ample
imperial images that disguise your truth.

from New Poets 1959

By ferry to the island

We crossed by ferry to the bare island
where sheep and cows stared coldly through the wind –
the sea behind us with its silver water,
the silent ferryman standing in the stern
clutching his coat about him like old iron.

We landed from the ferry and went inland
past a small church down to the winding shore
where a white seagull fallen from the failing
chill and ancient daylight lay so pure
and softly breasted that it made more dear

the lesser white around us. There we sat
sheltered by a rock beside the sea.
Someone made coffee, someone played the fool
in a high rising voice for two hours.
The sea's language was more grave and harsh.

And one sat there whose dress was white and cool.
The fool sparkled his wit that she might hear
new diamonds turning on her naked finger.
What might the sea think or the dull sheep
lifting its head through heavy Sunday sleep?

And, later, going home, a moon rising
at the end of a cart-track, minimum of red,
the wind being dark, imperfect cows staring
out of their half-intelligence, and a plough
lying on its side in the cold, raw

naked twilight, there began to move
slowly, like heavy water in the heart
the image of the gull and of that dress,
both being white and out of the darkness rising
the moon ahead of us with its rusty ring.

from Thistles and Roses 1961

For the unknown seamen of the 1939-45 war
Buried in Iona Churchyard

One would like to be able to write something for them
not for the sake of the writing but because
a man should be named in dying as well as living,
in drowning as well as on death-bed, and because
the brain being brain must try to establish laws.

Yet these events are not amenable
to any discipline that we can impose
and are not in the end even imaginable.
What happened was simply this, bad luck for those
who have lain here twelve years in a changing pose.

These things happen and there's no explaining,
and to call them 'chosen' might abuse a word.
It is better also not to assume a mourning,
moaning stance. These may well have concurred
in whatever suddenly struck them through the absurd

or maybe meaningful. One simply doesn't
know enough, or understand what came
out of the altering weather in a fashioned
descriptive phrase that was common to each name
or may have surrounded each like a dear frame.

Best not to make much of it and leave these seamen
in the equally altering acre they now have
inherited from strangers though yet human.
They fell from sea to earth, from grave to grave,
and, griefless now, taught others how to grieve.

from New Poets 1959

The visit of the inspectors

The inspectors come to inspect.
The inspected wait by their beds.

The trumpets sound. Man is on his way
through a tangle of paper, through a forest of pens,
through a trembling of cloth.
The inspectors fasten a button.
The inspectors notice a 2
missing from a memorandum
about what is expected from
an old typewriter
in the atomic age.

The office cleaner is hidden in a cupboard
because she is dirty
and smells like a cloud of dung
when you approach her:
similarly the office clerk
who has been here for fifty years
and reports absurd tales
of loyalty, honesty, sincerity,
who is, in relation to the inspectors,
indecipherable blotting paper.

Stand by your beds!
Hear the notes of the paper bugles
The shepherds on the green hillsides
spit lazily as they talk.
Soon they will be unable to play
For the paper mounts and mounts
and the illiterate inspectors
have their notebooks open.

Ah, poor shepherds, stand by your sheep!
You have to account for every moment
you dozed there, absorbing the sun.
And also those times you played cards
when you should have been watching
the position of the grass in the field,
and noting the temperature.

What have you done with your flutes?
The inspectors will want to know.
They are not educated men
but they know what they like
such as scenes showing harvests
and men toiling beautifully under the sun.
They will not speak proper grammar
and they wear blue shiny suits
and finally let me tell you they hate you
for being so idle.

They don't know anything about sheep
but they know about inspections
and their words are as definite as death.
They use language differently from you. Know that.
They do not suffer as you do
but they are human.

Your job therefore is to watch them
standing there with straws in your mouths.
Remember the blue suits, the thin wives,
the ladders of diamonds.
Remember it and put it in your music
which should be solid as the stones
that lie out on the hillsides
and after all ought to be here
when you are both gone.

from Lines Review no. 29, June 1969

Culloden and after

You understand it? How they returned from Culloden
over the soggy moors aslant, each cap
at the low ebb no new full tide could pardon:
how they stood silent at the end of the rope
unwound from battle: and to the envelope
of a bedded room came home, polite and sudden.

And how, much later, bards from Tiree and Mull
would write of exile in the hard town
where mills belched English, anger of new school:
how they remembered where the sad and brown
landscapes were dear and distant as the crown
that fuddled Charles might study in his ale.

There was a sleep. Long fences leaned across
the vacant croft. The silly cows were heard
mooing their sorrow and their Gaelic loss.
The pleasing thrush would branch upon a sword.
A mind withdrew against its dreamed hoard
as whelks withdraw or crabs their delicate claws.

And nothing to be heard but songs indeed
while wandering Charles would on his olives feed
and from his Minch of sherries mumble laws.

from Thistles and Roses 1961

A young Highland girl studying poetry

Poetry drives its lines into her forehead
like an angled plough across a bare field.
I've seen her kind before, of the live and dead
who bore humped creels when the beating winds were wild.

Nor did they know much poetry but were skilful
at healing children, bringing lambs to birth.
The earth they lived from did not make them soulful.
The foreign rose abated at their mouth.

177

Yet they were dancers too and feared the season
when 'pale Orion shook the seas with fire'.
Peculiar waters had their inner reasons
for curing wastrels of a mental star.

And she – like them – should grow along these valleys
bearing bright children, being kind to love.
Simple affection needs no complex solace
nor quieter minds abstractions of the grave.

For most must walk though some by natural flying
learn from the bitter winds a kind of praise.
These fruits are different. She will know one dying
but he by many deaths will bless her days.

from Thistles and Roses 1961

Envoi

Remember me when you come into your kingdom.
Remember me, beggar of mirrors, when you are confirmed
in the sleep of fulfilment on the white pillow.

Remember me who knock at the window,
who hirple on my collapsing stick, and know
the quivering northern lights of nerves.

Remember me in your good autumn.
I in my plates of frost go
among the falling crockery of hills

stones, plains, all falling and falling.
In my winter of the sick glass remember
me in your autumn, in your good sleep.

from The Law and the Grace 1965

Old woman

Your thorned back
heavily under the creel
you steadily stamped the rising daffodil.

Your set mouth
forgives no-one, not even God's justice
perpetually drowning law with grace.

Your cold eyes
watched your drunken husband come
unsteadily from Sodom home.

Your grained hands
dandled full and sinful cradles.
You built for your children stone walls.

Your yellow hair
burned slowly in a scarf of grey
wildly falling like the mountain spray.

Finally you're alone
among the unforgiving brass,
the slow silences, the sinful glass.

Who never learned,
not even aging, to forgive
our poor journey and our common grave

while the free daffodils
wave in the valleys and on the hills
the deer look down with their instinctive skills,

and the huge sea
in which your brothers drowned sings slow
over the headland and the peevish crow.

from The Law and the Grace 1965

From Bourgeois Land (No. 12)

My Scottish towns with Town Halls and with courts,
with tidy flowering squares and small squat towers,
with steady traffic, the clock's cruising hours,
the ruined castles and the empty forts,

you are so still one could believe you dead.
Policemen stroll beneath the leaves and sun.
Pale bank clerks sit on benches after noon
totting the tulips, entering clouds in red.

And yet from such quiet places furies start.
Gauleiters pace by curtained windows, grass
absorbs the blood of mild philosophers.
Artists are killed for an inferior art.

Mad bank clerks bubble with a strange new world.
Insulted waiters take a fierce revenge.
Inside expanding cages aesthetes lunge
at cripples or despisers of the word.

Stout fleshy matrons send their pekinese
on wolfish expeditions and the night
is palpitant with howls. The scraggy throat
of some schoolmistress sways in a new breeze.

The butcher's hairy hand raises an axe.
White heads are neatly sliced like morning bread.
The errand boy rides whistling through the dead.
The scholar hacks at documents and books.

And skies are clearer than they ever were.
The haze has lifted. Fiction becomes fact.
Desire has seized at last the virgin Act.
And distant Belsen smokes in the calm air.

from From Bourgeois Land 1969

Notes

Edwin Muir

For Ann Scott-Moncrieff page 26
A memorial in the easy epistolary manner, this poem is quite different from any other Muir wrote. Ann Scott-Moncrieff, a fellow Orcadian, was the author of verse in the Orkney dialect, short stories and two delightful children's books, *Aboard the Bulger* (1935) and *Auntie Robbo* (1959). She died tragically young, 'an inheritor of unfulfilled renown'. She impressed Muir and others with her unspoiled charm, fearlessness and resolution in the face of ill-health.

The combat page 29
This strange poem was based on a dream. Muir, in his dream, saw the creatures as described in the poem. He could see from their look that 'they knew each other, that they had fought a countless number of times and after this battle would fight again, that each meeting would be the first meeting that the dark, patient animal would always be defeated, and that the bright fierce animal would always win'. In the poem the brown-eyed creature is defeated, but escapes death and, later, returns to fight again.

The poem is symbolic and readers can read their own meaning into it. Muir wrote it in Prague, after February 1948, when the Communists seized power and crushed any opposition. The poem can represent human freedom again and again crushed by brutal force, but always rising again. Freedom was won by Czechoslovakia in 1918; brute force of the Nazis crushed it in 1938; freedom was regained in 1945; it was lost when the Communists seized power in 1948; freedom was beginning to assert itself in 1968, only to be crushed once more by Russian tanks in August 1968. Or the poem can be taken to represent the struggle of the individual soul against the processes of depersonalisation in the West as well as in Eastern Europe. Or it may represent the never-ending struggle between good and evil. The poem has such power that few readers are satisfied with the surface meaning of a fight between two animals.

The horses page 34

Muir suggests here that, by the way he has made use of his inventions, his radios, warships, aeroplanes and tractors . . ., man has sacrificed himself to a mechanical world and lost touch both with Nature, and with *his* own true nature. The outcome is a terrifying catastrophe, possibly the result of a nuclear war. The poem however does not treat this in detail but rather deals with hope, with a rebirth, a return to Nature and to an understanding of man's true self.

Man's destruction of a God-given world in a *seven day* war is an ironic answer to God's creation; the silence of ruin in place of the peace of accomplishment. But man as well as destroying his fellow men, has eliminated the industrial ugliness which perverted his soul. It is time for the re-assertion of nature, the restoration of the bond between Man and the Animal. Man is compelled to rediscover a simpler way of life. The returning horses remind us of Roy Campbell's *Horses of the Camargue.*

Hugh MacDiarmid

The diversity of MacDiarmid's work is the theme of the selection printed here. The first seven poems exemplify the early cry, the sudden (apparently unconscious) mastery of a language which was not his own native spoken Scots, but was an amalgam of this with dictionary-learned forms which are mixed indiscriminately throughout his work. At its best, represented by the short lyric 'Empty Vessel', this gift produces work of an intensity really beautiful, and in addition untranslatable. It is possible baldly to state the meaning of most of the poetry (indeed the poet himself frequently does this at public poetry-readings) yet the overtones are lost, and of course the lyric nature of the poetry destroyed by 'translation'. In the poem the mother's loss is so enormous as to dwarf the scale of any possible comparison, yet the low-keyed imagery and language keep this emotion within the poet's own limitations and emphasise (by contrast) the finality and the utterness of the loss of the child. These early lyrics, satirical, witty, serious, thoughtful, wild, achieve at their best something quite new in twentieth-century Scottish poetry.

Sic transit gloria Scotia page 41

Considered by many to be the peak of MacDiarmid's achievement, this poem in the form of a long constantly-shifting dramatic monologue, explores the varying thoughts of a drunken Scot who addresses the thistle – a complex image of Scotland – and comments on the present state of the country. In the passage printed, the drunk man's thoughts run from the gradual decay of himself and whisky in general (stanzas 1-5) to the corresponding decay of Scotland (stanzas 6-9) thanks to the decline of its culture (stanza 8), the indiscriminate exploitation of its past (stanza 10) and the sentimental and largely ignorant Burns cult (stanzas 11-14) which the drunk man holds in especial horror. The complex allusions of the first two lines of stanza 9 sum up the drunk man's feeling that Scotland has changed in character and that the past is irrevocably cut off from this century's culture. In stanza 15 the poet goes on to consider a more political set of values-in-decay with the criticisms of Christianity and the complex (and largely phoney) connections between Burns-club 'brotherhood' and present-day notions of brotherhood and equality. The one abiding idea is the drunk man's assurance of Burns's complete superiority to his present-day followers (stanzas 18, 21, 22). He is so 'dead dune' as to be unsure of anything else – even where he is (stanza 25). His quasi- (not always quasi-, but sometimes alert) philosophising may therefore ramble freely between countries and cultures without seeming disconnected, permitting MacDiarmid to draw freely on his erudition. All things point mercilessly to the degenerate state of Scotland and the Scottish people, for great poets, even Burns, may 'cheenge folks' talk but no' their natures, fegs!' (stanza 30). The range of the poem (like its length) is immense and brilliantly sustained. The subtlety of the illustrative material, and the linking of ideas, is well shown by MacDiarmid's treatment of Eliot in stanza 28. A form of 'A Drunk Man' enabled him to avoid the necessity of a coherent train of thought, the last thing to expect from a drunk man, and to use the width of the material and its ever-changing nature, to the best.

Other poems
The remaining poems, given the context of the ideas expounded before, make sense as a proper development of the early lyric poems. Not abstract 'chopped-up prose', they show a diverse nature using *all poetic forms* (Scottish and English, rhythmical and 'free') to explore the huge body of ideas which interest him, asserting the self which was arising in *A Drunk Man* to dominate the more self-effacing poet of the early lyrics. Politics, social questions, nationalism come to the fore as important features – an ardent Communist and self-confessed Anglophobe, MacDiarmid has been a contentious public figure for almost fifty years – and the poems show the self-developed genius in many moods, using the multiplicity of his gift to exploit the enormous diversity of life.

Stony limits page 51

Much of the character of MacDiarmid's mature work may be seen in a finely-developed form in this poem. The form of an elegy for a lost friend is particularly suitable to this poem, as it permits not only the public praising of a great figure, but also the public exploration of the poet's own character in trying to trace the reasons for his admiration of Doughty. These two functions of the poem form an easy balance, and sustain the interest of the reader despite the relatively 'flat' versification, the absence of conventional poetic beauty. This is the secret of MacDiarmid's mature verse and its appeal; gone completely are the extreme felicities of language which marked the earlier work, and in their place is a strenuous intellectual pattern which offers quite another attraction to the listener or reader. This idea is explicitly stated in 'The White Rose of Scotland', which rejects formal beauty for intellectual challenge. 'Stony Limits' exists to praise Doughty's exceptional qualities of sincerity and diversity of talent; these are the ostensible reasons for the panegyric. Doughty's greatness is such that MacDiarmid thinks of him in cosmic terms – Doughty's greatness and the greatness of the world are two ideas which, while not precisely linked, bind the imagery of the poem together. These are the twin organising ideas, and form the framework which attracts the later MacDiarmid, whose scientific interests are wide-ranging, and who uses every area of modern language for poetic expression. Here geological terms are freely used to indicate the scale of the comparison, and the timelessness of Doughty's greatness in MacDiarmid's eyes. The world is huge, Doughty almost as huge; beside him MacDiarmid, still alive, feels his physical smallness, and his intellectual greatness, and it is in the shifting awareness of this problem of scale that the most complex and successful elements of expression in the poem may be found.

George Bruce

Homage to El Greco page 70

This poem owes its power to the impact made on the poet by a study of 'The Agony in the Garden' by the late sixteenth-century painter, El Greco. The inspiration comes directly from the painting which is vividly translated into verbal rhythmic terms. Very noticeable are the quick impressions of the first section – the phrases describing the power and pathos of the setting, with the focus moving to the hands and eyes of Christ. The second section has both an immediacy and a dramatic quality – 'Look there'; and it quickly gathers up the raw material of Gethsemane, the geological world growth epitomised by the garden, to emphasise the cosmic power behind Christ's agony. All this leads to the third section with its short, prayer-like liturgical lines that give the inner message and throw the emphasis back to the centrepiece of the painting – the eyes and hands of Christ.

Structure, technique and theme are closely linked in this poem. One notes how the quick non-sentence technique is used to give the first impression of the scene, how the more formal sentence spreads over the second section to describe the garden in startlingly cosmic style, and how finally in the last section the change in the rhythm, the shortness of the lines, the repetition of linguistic patterns, the close-up technique, are all used to present the inner theme.

Death mask of a fisherman page 72

In the first section, the poet's imagined dead father comes alive to him, not in the mere physical appearance of the body, but in a 'look', a 'mask'. The rhythm here is clearly moving towards the poem's centre – a contemplation of the mystery of death, the 'unanswered question'. The second section gives an impression of the fast approaching death in terms of the disintegration and dissolution of the body. The imagery of shells and worms is appropriate here especially when thrown alongside the references to sea and storm; but the movement of this section too is towards the mystery – what the eyes suggested of the coming world beyond death. The third section in a series of phrase-references – to feature, skull, cheek, 'hollows' – presents the physical aspect of death vividly and immediately alongside the other aspect, the spiritual. Here the poet's understanding is deepened by a reference to art – to a face painted by El Greco in which this ethereal aspect is reflected. The last line spins out the idea of the indefinable quality of this aspect.

This poem illustrates the two influences working on the poetry of George Bruce – the background of sea life and the illuminating power of great art in interpreting life.

Visit in winter page 76

This is an ironic fantasy in which the poet contrasts the apparent unreality of the tail-coated white shirt-fronted Highland waiter with the *seemingly* more real Southern visitors who come to Scotland on short visits to kill game and whose actions do not appear rational. While behind the stiff shirt there is substance, of the here-today gone-tomorrow sportsmen, only the smoking guns really exist.

Laötian Peasant Shot page 77
Here George Bruce achieves the compression of technique found in
William Carlos Williams, the American poet, whom he admires.

Norman MacCaig

Byre page 97
This poem is typical of MacCaig, since the scene is presented as the
poet saw it, in a particular mood. It is impossible to separate the
scene from the poet – the reader sees the byre through the eyes,
feeling and attitudes of the poet. He has chosen to write a poem
about what is usually considered ordinary and commonplace, but he
has managed to throw over (it) a certain colouring of the imagination, whereby ordinary things should be presented to the mind in
an unusual aspect, as Wordsworth claimed to do in his poems.

In this poem he is 'praising things'. To MacCaig there is something holy, something sacred about the life of a croft, represented by
the byre:

> The thatched roof rings like heaven where mice
> Squeak small hosannahs all night long.

In these lines, too, there is a surprising paradox in the contrast
between words like 'thatched', 'mice', 'squeak', and the expressions
'rings like Heaven', 'hosannahs'. Again in the third stanza, describing the cows, the word 'mincing' strongly contrasts with the
expressions, 'vast presences' and 'swagbellied Aphrodites' (Greek
goddess of love and beauty). Throughout the poem there are com-
bined a devotional feeling, a sense of humour and a delighted appreciation of the details of the scene as he saw them:

the kittens

> . . . are tawny brooches
> Splayed on the chests of drunken sacks

and

> . . . miaow in circles, stalking
> With tail and hindleg one straight line.

This poem is written in English, but it is typically and tradition-
ally Scottish in its appreciation of life on a croft, its loving feeling for
animals, its brand of humour, its intimacy, warmth and homeliness.

A man in Assynt page 100
This is the first 72 lines of a poem of 271 lines. The poem was
commissioned by the BBC and transmitted with accompanying film in

the winter of 1967. Both poem and film deal with Western Sutherland inland from Lochinver.

At the beginning the poet gives the scene, naming the mountains of Assynt. Then he proceeds to give a vivid impression of the area, its landscape, its wild life, its people. This is no mere description since he deals with the region, not merely in space, but in time also. The first lines refer to the remote past and the processes which produced the landscape as we now see it. Then there is the historical background. After the 1745 Jacobite Rebellion the ancient civilisation of the Highlands of Scotland was destroyed. Clan chiefs were transformed into landowners. The chiefs-turned-lairds, thinking only of quick profits, began the systematic eviction of the crofters, to set up vast sheep farms, so that they could profit from the high prices then paid for wool. When imports lowered the price of wool, 'deer forests' for hunting actually became more profitable than sheep farms, and the rate of change was greatly increased. During the first six years of the nineteenth century over 15 000 people were made homeless in the sparsely populated Highlands of Scotland.

This is the historical background that MacCaig has in mind throughout the whole poem, and in the lines:

> . . . And man becomes,
> in this most beautiful corner of the land,
> one of the rare animals.

He ends the complete poem with a tentative hope:

> That sad withdrawal of people may, too,
> reverse itself and flood
> the bays and sheltered glens
> with new generations replenishing the land
> with its richest of riches – and coming, at last,
> into their own again.

Thus the poem is a combination of description and reflection, written in an easier, less concentrated style than in many of his other poems – to suit its original purpose of being heard and immediately understood rather than read.

Hotel room, 12th floor page 103

Here MacCaig sees the uncivilising process of the present technological advances in the same light as, but on a much larger scale than, the incursions of the Red Indian, in the nineteenth century, on the outposts of the Western progress of the white man.

Sydney Goodsir Smith

Epistle to John Guthrie page 105
The first volume of poetry by Sydney Goodsir Smith contained poems in English and poems in Scots, but his later poems were written in Scots. He deliberately chose to write in Scots rather than in English, justifying his choice in this poem, in his first published volume of poems *Skail Wind* 1941. The verse epistle is a traditional Scottish verse form used by Burns, Fergusson and others; such poems were written in an easy, relaxed style, to give the impression of someone speaking informally, as Smith does in this poem.

He deals with a very controversial topic. Some Scots, like Edwin Muir, maintain that the future of Scottish poetry is in the English language. Many others argue strongly for the use of Scots as the medium of Scottish poetry.

In this poem Smith argues for his choice of language. He maintains that Scots is a living, spoken language that can be the basis of poetry. But he also points out that poets create their own language for their purposes, and that this may be very different from the spoken language, an inadequate medium for what the poet wants to say. He refers to the language of Shakespeare's *King Lear*, the language of Burns ('Rantin', rovin' Robin'), Gavin Douglas (*c.* 1474-1522), William Dunbar (?1460-?1521), Keats's 'Ode to a Nightingale'; and comes to the conclusion that, for him, Scots has more vitality, since

> English . . . 's near deid,

which may remind us that T. S. Eliot, writing about the same time, spoke of the language as

> . . . shabby equipment always deteriorating
> In the general mess of imprecision of feeling.

Largo page 108
Largo, a small fishing village in Fife, on the Firth of Forth, about ten miles south of St Andrews, used to have a flourishing fishing industry, but this has been destroyed. The poem was written of 1939, when only one drifter was left of the fleet of fishing boats.

Here is a good example of the poet's achievement in his best lyrics, many of which are love poems with the singing voice, and controlled intensity which makes these lyrics memorable. The poem begins with the slow sad movement of the largo of a piece of music, as the poet paints the scene with the last boat fishing from this shore. The movement quickens in the other stanzas as the poet passionately protests against the impersonal forces of the contemporary world which have destroyed the good life of sturdy independence at Largo, till he reaches the climax of the last two lines:

> Whan yon lane boat I see,
> Daith and rebellion blinn ma ee!

King and Queen o the four airts page 110
Essentially a youthful poem, the remarkable singing quality of the first five stanzas overshadows somewhat the more serious final verses which bring us back to the reality of life for the ordinary man in Scotland in the depressed 1930s. The honest man, *pace* Burns, the real King o' men without even home, is happier than all the Kings with their Holyroods and Xanadus. The poem shows Goodsir Smith's delight in language with characteristic hyperbole and the use of proper names for emotive and literary effect.

Edwin Morgan

Aberdeen train page 130
A moment of illumination to the poet as he passes through the work-a-day world of the Mearns (farmland around Stonehaven). From the misty Chinese painting before him in the dim carriage window the poet turns to the philosophical idea that nothing is unimportant.

In the snack-bar page 132
The drabness of the scene and the squalor of the subject here are apt to obscure the poet's art. Is the steady progress of the blind hunchback cripple negotiating the many snares of slidy puddles, the spilt sugar and looming chairs not, on its own scale, to be compared with the skilled climber encountering the Ice Fall on Mount Everest?

Che page 135
A tribute to Ernesto 'Che' Guevara (1928-1968), Argentinian comrade of Fidel Castro and fellow founder of the new Cuba. Guevara was first a doctor and then guerilla leader. He wrote a book in 1960 on *Guerilla Warfare* after the success of the Cuban Revolution. He was brutally murdered in the jungle, fighting against Bolivian tyranny. His writing and example have inspired the oppressed throughout the world. The poet saw the smile of the dead man in a newspaper photograph.

189

Canedolia page 136
In this poem the reader is taken on a lexical dream tour of Scotland. The metathesis of the title spills over into the fuddled confusion of double-barrelled place names in lines 30-35. The poet here explores humorously the strangely evocative association qualities of place names. There is a reward, but no prize, for tracing all the places mentioned in the poem.

King Billy page 138
Line 11 *red, white, blue and gold* are the colours of Protestant Orangemen. Line 15 *King Billy* – Billy Fullarton was the gang leader who died, aged 57, in 1962. The gang was named the Billy Boys after William of Orange. Line 19 *sherrickings* – see chapter 5 of the novel *No Mean City*. A *sherricking* is a public showing-up in which none can foretell the consequence. It often resulted in a bloody battle with razors, boots and fists. Line 23 *Conks* – Roman Catholic gang. Line 25 *Sillitoe* – Sir Percy Sillitoe, Chief Constable of Glasgow in the early 1930s, broke up the gangs.

From the domain of Arnheim page 139
A science-fiction poem influenced by the short story *The Domain of Arnheim* 1847 by Edgar Allan Poe (1809-1849) and the surrealist paintings by the Belgian painter René Magritte (1893-1963), also *Le Domaine d'Arnheim* (1949). 'There *may* be a class of beings, human once, but now invisible to humanity, to whom, from afar, our disorder may seem order – our unpicturesqueness picturesque' (E. A. Poe, 'The Domain of Arnheim'). In the poem time travellers, seeing but unseen by the observed, land from their space ship in an ice-age scene. A similar approach to this subject is made in H. G. Wells's *The Time Machine* 1895.

Alexander Scott

Haar in Princes Street page 142
In the capital city, enveloped in mist, the poet sees the purposelessness and uncertainty of aim in Scotland today. History frowns on the present.

Calvinist sang page 143
An expression of a puritanical view of the world of pleasure, satirical of course.

Big beat page 149
In this poem the author humorously expresses his perplexity at the on-goings of a particularly noisy TV pop programme he was un-

fortunate enough to view. The wee lass with the hoarse quavering-voice, the three buxom baby-faced blondes, and the unhealthy-looking melancholy youth yelling his head off, all arouse the scorn of the poet who ends his strictures with a mock-serious prayer in the fifteenth-century manner – 'O wash awa this weird!'

Doun wi dirt! page 150
This original flyting derives from the scatological works of the undernoted authors:

Marquis de Sade (1740-1814)
  Justine ou les Malheurs de la Vertu 1791 etc.
Leopold Von Sacher-Masoch (1836-1895)
  The Legend of Cain 1870-7 *False Ermine* 1873
Frank Harris (1856-1931)
  My Life 1926
James Joyce (1882-1941)
  Ulysses 1922
D. H. Lawrence (1885-1930)
  Sons and Lovers 1913 *Lady Chatterley's Lover* 1928
Henry Miller (b. 1891)
  Tropic of Cancer 1934 *Tropic of Capricorn* 1938
Jean Genet (b. 1910)
  The Maids 1949 *The Balcony* 1958
William Burroughs (b. 1914)
  The Naked Lunch 1959
Sydney Goodsir Smith (b. 1915)
  Under the Eildon Tree 1948, *Carotid Cornucopius* 1964
Alexander Trocchi
  Young Adam 1961, *Cain's Book* 1963
Alan Sharp (b. 1934)
  A Green Tree in Gedde 1965, *The Wind Changes* 1967

The non-committal conclusion to the poem may be interpreted 'Present company not excepted (or accepted)'.

Von Braun p. 153
Werner Von Braun (b. 1912) was a German rocketry expert who developed the V-2 rocket used against Britain in 1945. Since the end of the Second World War he has been closely involved in the US Space programme. Line 5, the US captain, on first circuit of the moon was reading from the book of Genesis.

George Mackay Brown

Snow: from a hospital page 159

The poet in hospital muses on snow and its meaning for him. First it brings ill health. The snow is alien, from another planet, but none the less real. He prefers the wispy Chinese picture of snow. 'The bronchial tree loaded with the white birds of winter' means that his tubes are congested and whistling with phlegm.

He longs for summer warmth to bring an end to the winds and snow of winter, as the return of Odysseus brought an end to the apparently never-ending weaving and unravelling of Penelope's web. The intense light coming from the snow illuminates with unnatural clarity the poet's experience. In this heightened state he looks on the world as a place of tapestry and legend, remote, timeless and unreal. Yet he is in hospital and his suffering is real. In the world outside the snowman, picturesque and superficially lovable, carries the symbolism of the cruelty of winter.

The heavenly stones page 161

This takes the form of a narrative from the mouth of Christ as a child looking into the future. The three men combine elements of the Magi and the Temptation in the Wilderness. All the symbolic stones are heavenly if treated in the right way. Gold and red at first are temptations but if the third stone is accepted, the others are transfigured and become heavenly as well. 'The dancing five' represent the five senses. The 'beggar's clout' suggests a life of poverty. The other mantle offers the possibility of a worldly, rather than heavenly, kingdom with even more beautiful women than Solomon had in his Court. It should be remembered here that 'The Song of Solomon', allegorised, is the Love of Christ. The 'bitters' are all the consequences of the fall of Adam, the fruit which has grown on the tree of life since Adam's expulsion from Eden. 'You will hang on your own tree', is, of course, the Crucifixion. 'The grape of God' represents the slow growth through 4004 years from Adam's fall to the Crucifixion, of the Tree of Life by which Adam fell and on which Christ redeemed the world. 'The five gates of your blood' represents the Five Wounds of Christ, in his hands, his feet and his side. 'The man of dust will . . . eat your flesh' etc. suggests the Eucharist, the bread being the body of Christ and the wine the blood. 'That hour I felt mortality Fasten about my bones . . . and heaven leaked from the stones' symbolises the Incarnation of Christ with which comes the transfiguration of the Gold and the World of the Senses. From the shaking of the Apple from the Tree of Life, the Voice of God in the Garden of Eden, the Flaming Sword and the seductiveness of Eve comes the Fall of Man.

At this point, the boy Christ hears his mother at the hearth calling him and he observes his father, the Carpenter, at work, from the same trees fashioning the Crib of birth and the Cross on which Christ was to suffer. Then he sees the temporal power of Rome passing swiftly away. The vision over, Christ throws away the stones with which he has been playing and returns to his childhood divinity. The Historical Christ may be taken here as the Universal Christ in Everyman.

These notes are provided to show one interpretation of this complex poem. The biblical and allegorical references can be interpreted in several ways, and the complexity of this poem is a reflection of George Herbert's influence on Mackay Brown.

Iain Crichton Smith

John Knox page 172
This sonnet concerns the conflict between the austere Calvinist Knox and the pleasure-loving Mary Queen of Scots. The struggle is symbolised in the assault upon the sophisticated, corrupt yet tender and feminine world of Mary by the absolute sword and the elemental forces of storm, thunder and lightning associated with Knox.

from 'Seagulls' page 172
The seagull is a recurrent image in Crichton Smith's poetry. On this occasion the poet is reflecting on the separateness of all living things from every other. The true nature of the seagull can only be guessed at remotely by man.

By ferry to the island page 173
Here there is the contrast of light and dark, the picnickers enjoying simple pleasures with the Charon-like figure of the ferryman looking on, and farther off 'the sea's language . . . grave and harsh.'

The visit of the inspectors page 175
The inspectors can refer to army officers inspecting soldiers, or school inspectors, or might be taken as bureaucrats, in a modern age, looking with myopic eyes, only at what they want to see, mechanically following a routine, uninterested in what is beneath the surface. They ignore people and the things which truly matter in life.

A young Highland girl studying poetry page 177
The girl in the poem is one of a race of women who embody the qualities the poet most admires in the Hebrideans; stoicism in the face of the stern elements, quiet practical skills and a natural easy happiness in love. Her puzzled frown is ample indication that poetry for poetry's sake is not for this girl.

Old woman page 179
(cf. 'The Old Woman' of George Mackay Brown.) This clear but symbol-packed poem is of one who never possessed charity. She stamps upon the rising daffodil, a symbol (also in 'Poem of Lewis') of natural beauty, disapproves even of God's mercy and regards her children as conceived in sin, not love. She cramps them within her narrow faith. Implicit is the poet's pity for the old woman now she is alone with nothing.

BIBLIOGRAPHY

GENERAL READING

Kitchin, George. 'The Modern Makars'. In Kinsley, James (ed.). *Scottish Poetry: A Critical Survey*. Cassell 1955, pp. 256-79.
Wittig, Kurt. 'Breakers: The Scottish Renaissance. I. The Modern Makars'. In his *The Scottish Tradition in Literature*. Oliver & Boyd 1958, pp. 280-370.
Glen, Duncan. *Hugh MacDiarmid (Christopher Murray Grieve) and the Scottish Renaissance*. Chambers 1964.

ANTHOLOGIES

Macdiarmid, Hugh (ed.) *The Golden Treasury of Scottish Poetry*. Macmillan 1940.
Smith, J. C. and Oliver, J. W. (eds.) *A Scots Anthology: From the Thirteenth to The Twentieth Century*. Oliver & Boyd 1949.
Young, Douglas (ed.) *Scottish Verse, 1851-1951*. Nelson 1952.
Lindsay, Maurice (ed.) *Modern Scottish Poetry: An Anthology of The Scottish Renaissance*. 2nd ed. Faber 1966.
MacQueen, John and Scott, Tom (eds.) *The Oxford Book of Scottish Verse*. Oxford, Clarendon Press 1966.
Mackie, R. L. (ed.) *A Book of Scottish Verse*. (The World's Classics, 417) 2nd ed. rev. by Maurice Lindsay. Oxford University Press 1967.
Bruce, George (ed.) *The Scottish Literary Revival: An Anthology of Twentieth-Century Poetry*. Collier-Macmillan 1968.
MacCaig, Norman and Scott, Alexander (eds.) *Contemporary Scottish Verse, 1959-1969*. (The Scottish Library) Calder & Boyars 1970.
Glen, Duncan (ed.) *The Akros Anthology of Scottish Poetry, 1965-70*. Akros 1970.
Scott, Tom (ed.) *The Penguin Book of Scottish Verse*. Penguin 1970.

Akros (three times a year) first published 1965.
Lines Review (quarterly) first published 1952.
Scottish International (quarterly, now monthly) first published 1968.
Scottish Poetry (annually) first published 1966.
Studies in Scottish Literature (quarterly) first published 1963.

Edwin Muir

Collected Poems, 1921-58. 2nd ed. Faber 1964.
Selected Poems. Faber 1965.
An Autobiography. Hogarth Press 1954.
Essays on Literature and Society. Rev. ed. Hogarth Press 1965.

Butter, Peter. *Edwin Muir.* (Writers and Critics) Oliver & Boyd 1962.
Butter, Peter. *Edwin Muir: Man and Poet.* (Biography and Criticism, 7) Oliver & Boyd 1966.
Muir, Willa. *Belonging: A Memoir.* Hogarth Press 1968.

Hugh MacDiarmid

Collected Poems. Oliver & Boyd 1962. Rev. ed. Collier-Macmillan 1967.
A Lap of Honour. MacGibbon & Kee 1967.
A Clyack Sheaf. MacGibbon & Kee 1969.
More Collected Poems. MacGibbon & Kee 1970.
Craig, David and Manson, John (eds.) *Selected Poems.* (The Penguin Poets) Penguin 1970.
Buthlay, Kenneth (ed.) *The Uncanny Scot: A Selection of Prose.* MacGibbon & Kee 1968.
Glen, Duncan (ed.) *Selected Essays.* Cape 1969.
Lucky Poet: A Self-Study in Literature and Political Ideas. Methuen 1943.
The Company I've Kept. Hutchinson 1966.

Duval, K. D. and Smith, S. G. (eds.) *Hugh MacDiarmid: A Festschrift.* Duval 1962.
Buthlay, Kenneth. *Hugh MacDiarmid (C. M. Grieve)* (Writers and Critics) Oliver & Boyd 1964.
Glen, Duncan. *Hugh MacDiarmid (Christopher Murray Grieve) and the Scottish Renaissance.* Chambers 1964.
Smith, Iain Crichton. *The Golden Lyric: An Essay.* Akros 1967.

Weston, John C. *Hugh MacDiarmid's A Drunk Man Looks at the Thistle: An Essay*. Akros 1970.
Agenda. Vol. 5, no. 4-vol. 6, no. 1 (1967-8). Double issue: Hugh MacDiarmid and Scottish Poetry.
Akros nos. 13, 14 (1970) were issued simultaneously as a Hugh MacDiarmid issue.

William Soutar

Seeds in the Wind. Grant and Murray 1933. Rev. ed. Dakers 1943. Illustrated by Colin Gibson. Dakers 1948.
Poems in Scots. Moray Press 1935.
MacDiarmid, Hugh (ed.) *Collected Poems*. Dakers 1948.
Aitken, W. R. (ed.) *Poems in Scots and English*. Oliver & Boyd 1961.
Scott, Alexander (ed.) *Diaries of a Dying Man*. Chambers 1954.

Scott, Alexander. *Still Life: William Soutar, 1898-1943*. Chambers 1958.

George Bruce

Sea Talk. (Poetry Scotland Series, 2) Maclellan 1944.
Selected Poems. (Saltire Modern Poets) Oliver & Boyd 1947.
'*Landscapes and Figures: A Selection of Poems*.' Akros 1967.
Collected Poems. Edinburgh U.P. 1970.

Robert Garioch

Seventeen Poems for Sixpence (with Sorley Maclean). Chalmers Press 1940.
Chuckies on the Cairn. Chalmers Press 1949.
The Masque of Edinburgh. M. Macdonald 1954.
Selected Poems. M. Macdonald 1966.

Norman MacCaig

Far Cry. Routledge 1943.
The Inward Eye. Routledge 1946.
Riding Lights. Hogarth Press 1955.
The Sinai Sort. Hogarth Press 1957.
A Common Grace. Hogarth Press 1960.
A Round of Applause. Hogarth Press 1962.

Measures. Hogarth Press 1965.
Surroundings. Hogarth Press 1966.
Rings on a Tree. Hogarth Press 1968.
A Man in My Position. Hogarth Press 1969.
Selected Poems. Hogarth Press 1970.

Akros No. 7 (1968) was a Norman MacCaig issue.

Sydney Goodsir Smith

Skail Wind. Chalmers Press 1941.
The Wanderer and other Poems. Oliver & Boyd 1943.
The Deevil's Waltz. Maclellan 1946.
Selected Poems. (Saltire Modern Poets) Oliver & Boyd 1947.
So Late into the Night: Fifty Lyrics 1944-8. Peter Russell 1952.
Cokkils. M. Macdonald 1953.
Under the Eildon Tree. Serif Books 1948. 2nd ed. 1954.
Omens: Nine Poems. M. Macdonald 1955.
Orpheus and Euridice: A Dramatic Poem. M. Macdonald 1955.
Figs and Thistles. Oliver & Boyd 1959.
The Wallace: A Triumph in Five Acts. Oliver & Boyd 1960.
*Carotid Cornucopius, Caird of the Cannon Gait and Voyeur of
the Outlook Tower*. Caledonian Press 1947. Rev. ed. M. Macdonald
1964.
Kynd Kittock's Land. M. Macdonald 1965.
The Vision of the Prodigal Son. M. Macdonald 1966.
Fifteen Poems and a Play. Southside 1969.

Akros No. 10 (May 1969) was a Sydney Goodsir Smith issue.

Tom Scott

Seeven Poems o Maister Francis Villon made owre intil Scots.
Peter Russell 1953.
An Ode til a New Jerusalem. M. Macdonald 1956.
The Ship, and Ither Poems. Oxford U.P. 1963.
'At the Shrine o the Unkent Sodger: a Poem for Recitation'.
Akros 1968.
Dunbar: A Critical Exposition of the Poems. Oliver & Boyd 1966.

Alexander Scott

The Latest in Elegies. Caledonian Press 1949.
Selected Poems. (Saltire Modern Poets) Oliver & Boyd 1950.

198

Untrue Thomas: A Play in One Act. Caledonian Press 1952.
Mouth Music: Poems and Diversions. M. Macdonald 1954.
'Cantrips'. Akros 1968.

Edwin Morgan

The Cape of Good Hope. Peter Russell 1955.
Gnomes. Akros 1968.
The Second Life: Selected Poems. Edinburgh U.P. 1968.
Penguin Modern Poets, 15. Alan Bold, Edward Braithwaite, Edwin Morgan. Penguin 1969.
The Horseman's Word: a Sequence of Concrete Poems. Akros 1972.
Parkland Poets, 5.
Twelve Songs. Castlelaw Press 1970.
The Whittrick: A Poem in Eight Dialogues. Akros 1970.

George Mackay Brown

The Storm, and Other Poems. Orkney Press 1954.
Loaves and Fishes. Hogarth Press 1959.
The Year of the Whale. Hogarth Press 1965.
A Calendar of Love and Other Stories. Hogarth Press 1967.
A Time to Keep and Other Stories. Hogarth Press 1969.
An Orkney Tapestry. Gollancz 1969.
A Spell for Green Corn. (Play) Hogarth Press 1970.
Fishermen with Ploughs: A Poem Cycle. Hogarth Press 1971.

Iain Crichton Smith

The Long River. M. Macdonald 1955.
Thistles and Roses. Eyre & Spottiswoode 1961.
Deer in the High Hills. Giles Gordon 1962.
The Law and the Grace. Eyre & Spottiswoode 1965.
Consider the Lilies. (Novel) Gollancz 1968; Pergamon 1970.
Ben Dorain. Translated from the Gaelic of Duncan Ban Macintyre. Akros 1969.
From Bourgeois Land. Gollancz 1969.
The Last Summer. (Novel) Gollancz 1969.
Survival without Error, and other Stories. Gollancz 1970.
Selected Poems. Gollancz 1970.

Lines Review No. 29 (June 1969) was an Iain Crichton Smith issue.

INDEX OF FIRST LINES

201

ACKNOWLEDGMENTS

The editor and publishers thank the following for permission to reproduce copyright material:
George Bruce for his poems; Robert Garioch and M. Macdonald for their poems; Norman MacCaig and Hogarth Press Ltd for 'Summer farm' from *Riding Lights*, 'November night, Edinburgh' from *The Sinai Sort*, 'Nude in a fountain', 'Goat', 'Feeding ducks' and 'Edinburgh courtyard in July' from *A Common Grace*, 'Byre' from *A Round of Applause*, 'Assisi', 'Smuggler' and 'The streets of Florence' from *Surroundings*, 'Crossing the border' and 'Hotel room, 12th floor' from *Rings on a Tree*, 'A man in Assynt' from *A Man in my Position*; Hugh MacDiarmid for 'My quarrel with England', 'A drunk man' and 'Stony limits'; Hugh MacDiarmid and the Macmillan Company for 'The bonnie broukit bairn', 'The watergaw', 'Overinzievar', 'Crowdieknowe' 'O Jesu Parvule', 'Wheesht, wheesht', 'Empty vessel', 'Of John Davidson', 'On the ocean floor', 'After two thousand years', 'The kind of poetry I want' and 'The Caledonian Antisyzygy' from *Collected Poems 1962 and Collected Poems 1967*; George Mackay Brown for 'Unlucky boat', 'Snow', 'A warped boat', 'Winter bride' and 'Haddock fishermen'; George Mackay Brown and Hogarth Press Ltd for 'Our Lady of the waves', 'Old fisherman with guitar', 'Hamnavoe Market', 'The hawk' and 'Country girl' from *The Year of the Whale* and 'The heavenly stones' from *Loaves and Fishes*; Edwin Morgan for 'Shantyman' and 'Che'; Edwin Morgan and Edinburgh University Press for 'Aberdeen train', 'Trio', 'One cigarette', 'In the snack-bar', 'Canedolia', 'King Billy' and 'From the domain of Arnheim' from *The Second Life*; Faber and Faber Ltd for 'Childhood', 'Horses', 'The wayside station', 'Scotland 1941', 'The little general', 'For Ann Scott-Moncrieff', 'The labyrinth', 'The combat', 'The annunciation', 'One foot in Eden', 'Scotland's winter', 'To Franz Kafka' and 'The horses' from Edwin Muir's *Collected Poems 1921-1958*; Alexander

Scott for his poems; Tom Scott for 'Villanelle de Noël', 'Jay' and 'Auld Sanct Aundrians'; Tom Scott and Oxford University Press for 'Adam', 'Orpheus' and 'The bride' from *The Ship and Ither Poems*; Iain Crichton Smith for 'Some days were running legs' and 'Poem of Lewis'; Iain Crichton Smith and Eyre & Spottiswoode for 'John Knox', 'By ferry to the island', 'Culloden and after', 'A young Highland girl studying poetry' and 'Old woman' from *Thistles and Roses* and 'Envoi' from *The Law and the Grace*; Iain Crichton Smith and Gollancz for 'The visit of the inspectors', 'from "Seagulls" ' and 'For the unknown seamen' from *From Bourgeois Land*; Iain Crichton Smith and M. Macdonald for 'In Luss Churchyard' from *The Long River*; Iain Crichton Smith and *Lines Review* for the translation of 'Dain Do Eimhir'; Sydney Goodsir Smith for his poems; Sydney Goodsir Smith and Southside (Publishers) Ltd for *The Kenless Strand*; the Trustees of the National Library of Scotland for the poems by William Soutar; *Lines Review* for the Scots Style Sheet reproduced from No. 9, August 1955.